VOLUME 4

OLD TESTAMEN

THE NEW COLLEGEVILLE BIBLE COMMENTARY

LEVITICUS

J. Edward Owens, O.SS.T.

SERIES EDITOR

Daniel Durken, O.S.B.

LITURGICAL PRESS

Collegeville, Minnesota

www.litpress.org

Nihil Obstat: Reverend Robert Harren, *Censor deputatus.*
Imprimatur: ✛ Most Reverend John F. Kinney, J.C.D., D.D., Bishop of St. Cloud, Minnesota, December 17, 2010.

Design by Ann Blattner.

1	2	3	4	5	6	7	8	9

Library of Congress Cataloging-in-Publication Data

Owens, J. Edward.
    Leviticus / J. Edward Owens.
        p.   cm. — (The new Collegeville Bible commentary. Old Testament ; v. 4)
    ISBN 978-0-8146-2838-6
    1. Bible. O.T. Leviticus—Commentaries.   I. Title.

BS1255.53.O94   2011
222'.1307—dc22   2011013580

CONTENTS

ABBREVIATIONS

Books of the Bible

Acts—Acts of the Apostles
Amos—Amos
Bar—Baruch
1 Chr—1 Chronicles
2 Chr—2 Chronicles
Col—Colossians
1 Cor—1 Corinthians
2 Cor—2 Corinthians
Dan—Daniel
Deut—Deuteronomy
Eccl (or Qoh)—Ecclesiastes
Eph—Ephesians
Esth—Esther
Exod—Exodus
Ezek—Ezekiel
Ezra—Ezra
Gal—Galatians
Gen—Bible Book
Hab—Habakkuk
Hag—Haggai
Heb—Hebrews
Hos—Hosea
Isa—Isaiah
Jas—James
Jdt—Judith
Jer—Jeremiah
Job—Job
Joel—Joel
John—John
1 John—1 John
2 John—2 John
3 John—3 John
Jonah—Jonah
Josh—Joshua
Jude—Jude
Judg—Judges
1 Kgs—1 Kings

2 Kgs—2 Kings
Lam—Lamentations
Lev—Leviticus
Luke—Luke
1 Macc—1 Maccabees
2 Macc—2 Maccabees
Mal—Malachi
Mark—Mark
Matt—Matthew
Mic—Micah
Nah—Nahum
Neh—Nehemiah
Num—Numbers
Obad—Obadiah
1 Pet—1 Peter
2 Pet—2 Peter
Phil—Philippians
Phlm—Philemon
Prov—Proverbs
Ps(s)—Psalms
Rev—Revelation
Rom—Romans
Ruth—Ruth
1 Sam—1 Samuel
2 Sam—2 Samuel
Sir—Sirach
Song—Song of Songs
1 Thess—1 Thessalonians
2 Thess—2 Thessalonians
1 Tim—1 Timothy
2 Tim—2 Timothy
Titus—Titus
Tob—Tobit
Wis—Wisdom
Zech—Zechariah
Zeph—Zephaniah

The Book of Leviticus

Leviticus often seems a strange and antiquated book to the modern reader. Its prescriptions regarding cleanliness, diet, and liturgy hardly resonate with modern science, culture, and religion. However, it is noteworthy that the first chapters of Leviticus were traditionally a primer for Jewish children at the synagogue. The rationale for this choice deserves comment. Let the children who are pure learn about sacrifices that are pure. Let the pure begin their educational journey with what is holy, wholesome, and whole.

Although the modern reader may question such reasoning, I suggest that it bespeaks timeless pedagogical values on at least two levels. First, Leviticus teaches us to appreciate rules of right conduct based on clear and measurable standards. Small children have yet to understand abstract thinking and complex moral issues, so how "age appropriate" it is to introduce them to material of some catechetical nature, i.e., moral lessons about the fundamentals of one's religion. Second, education promotes ongoing cultural and religious values. What are the abiding canons of right conduct, liturgical integrity, accountability to the community, and building a better future for the next generation?

This is the stuff of Leviticus that speaks to the Old Testament theology of "teaching to remember" that begins with the exodus story of the first Passover: "When your children ask you, 'What does this rite of yours mean?' you will reply, 'It is the Passover sacrifice for the LORD, who passed over the houses of the Israelites in Egypt; when he struck down the Egyptians, he delivered our houses'" (Exod 12:26-27). The saga must ever be retold lest it be forgotten.

With the emergence of Judaism in the postexilic periods (the Persian [539–333 B.C.] and subsequent Greco-Roman period), preservation of Israel's heritage took on great importance. The Torah (the first five books of the Bible, also called the Pentateuch) became canonical. The Israelite monarchy had ended with the Babylonian exile and new groups assumed leadership roles in Judaism, among them the Sadducees, Pharisees, priests, scribes, and elders. The second temple cult held sway in Jerusalem, but the Diaspora Jews had the synagogues in communities outside of Palestine.

With such cultural and religious diversity, the saga of Israel as a people and nation had to be preserved. This agenda led to the designation of canonical books, i.e., the scriptural heritage that was inspired and authoritative as God's timeless word. The book of Leviticus played a role in this task via its preservation of liturgical, social, and other prescriptions that acknowledge God's holiness and seek to inculcate such holiness in the people.

Stylistically, Leviticus is dominated by laws and regulations pertaining to priest and laity. The Israelites are by definition a priestly people: "You will be to me a kingdom of priests, a holy nation. That is what you must tell the Israelites" (Exod 19:6). The narrative flows from the book of Exodus and leads into the book of Numbers. Moses is the chief spokesperson who receives revelations from the Lord at the tent of meeting (1:1). Moses calls all the people to holiness and to atone for ritual and personal sin. Holiness pervades all of life and is not limited to the realm of the sacred. Holiness flows through creation: from the tabernacle to the home, from the sacrificial offering to the fields where the grain and animals are raised.

These initial observations serve to orient the reader to this commentary. The book of Leviticus at first glance may seem dated, but it offers lessons for today. The ancients had different canons of purity, social contact, and religious observance. However, upon a closer reading of the text, their needs, motivations, and practices resonate with our own. Their God of the ancestors (Abraham, Isaac, and Jacob) is our God as well. Their intentionality to stand before God in sincerity and truth was as strong as ours. In sum, the book of Leviticus has much to teach us today once we grapple with its essential messages and apply them to our religious life.

The historical background of Leviticus

The books of the Hebrew Scriptures are designated by initial words in the text. Genesis is called *bĕrēʾshit*, *"In the beginning* [when God created the heavens and the earth]." Exodus is designated as *shĕmôt*, "[These are the] *names*." Leviticus is titled *wayyiqrāʾ*, "[The LORD] *called* [Moses]." The opening word "called" in Leviticus introduces a long speech wherein Moses speaks to the people of Israel regarding various laws and observances. The English title Leviticus comes from the Greek word *Levitikon*, i.e., what is levitical and priestly in nature. However, the Levites are mentioned but once in the book regarding the redemption of their houses at the jubilee year (25:32-34). Leviticus relates more to practices of the Israelites as a people than to duties of the Levites and priests.

Leviticus is dominated by the Priestly source/tradition (called P) that runs from Genesis into parts of Deuteronomy. This tradition highly influenced the final redaction of the Pentateuch. The literary and theological characteristics of the P tradition include attention to genealogies, laws, God's abiding presence in the midst of Israel, and the power of blessing. Sabbath rest, the Sinai covenant, and proper cultic observance are related themes. Further, the P tradition offers a lasting diatribe against pagan religion.

Pagan religion in the Scriptures is typically depicted as capricious, malevolent, and coercive of creation in general and humankind in particular. The gods demand to be fed, and sacrifices offered by humans serve to satisfy the gods' hunger and sometimes calm their rage. Demons are all around and affect many aspects of life. In pagan religions the celestial bodies were typically divine and maintained creation in its seasonal cycles.

The parade example of a P diatribe against such paganism is the description of the celestial bodies in Genesis 1, the six-day creation account after which God rests from work. Therein, the narrative describes a greater and lesser light in the heavens: "God made the two great lights, the greater one to govern the day, and the lesser one to govern the night; and the stars" (Gen 1:16). Neither object is named sun or moon; neither lamp does more than provide the light God had designated to it. The stars are mentioned almost in passing.

The P tradition demands monotheism and being holy as God is holy. Religious life must mirror the order and cyclic pattern seen in creation. Such order is not about dry legalism and forensic justice. To live well and stand sincerely before God bespeak peace (Hebrew *shālôm*). Peace means health, happiness, abundance, and a good name in the community: "May the LORD bless you from Zion, / may you see Jerusalem's prosperity / all the days of your life, / and live to see your children's children. / Peace upon Israel!" (Ps 128:5-6).

The P tradition evidences that all cultures hope to elicit the help of supernatural powers in controlling nature and society. Each religion has its unique ritual observances to that end. Humans seek to court or appease spiritual beings with sacrifices thought to be pleasing and appropriate. The ancient Israelites and their neighbors used animal and grain sacrifices for the most part. Some engaged in child sacrifice. Other cultures, such as Native American, offered tobacco and food to their spiritual entities. In many cultures the priest, shaman, or other figure often led the rituals in the hope of some good: a bountiful harvest, victory in warfare, or relief from a plague. Ancient Israel was much caught up in purity, atonement, and thanksgiving to their Lord. Festivals were also times of covenant renewal.

The P tradition reminds the contemporary reader that our religious world shares common ground with the ancients. We, too, are solicitous of liturgy that is valid, licit, and observed in its proper season. We embrace annual observances that characterize our religious heritage and bring the past alive in the present. Such practices as the Advent wreath, ashes on Ash Wednesday, fast and abstinence during Lent, fronds on Palm Sunday, and water at Easter come to mind. Certain phrases in Leviticus speak to every age and religion. These include "You shall love your neighbor as yourself" (19:18; see Luke 10:27) and "For I, the LORD, am your God. You shall make and keep yourselves holy, because I am holy" (11:44; see Matt 5:48).

In sum, I invite the reader of this commentary to look for timeless values and theological connections that transcend primitive science and time conditioned practices. Let us look to themes and motifs that make Leviticus a book still worth reading and a source of biblical-spiritual reflection in every age. To this end, I suggest that the reader begin by perusing the review aids and discussion topics at the end of the commentary.

The literary artistry of Leviticus

Recent biblical studies have given attention to fresh "lenses" through which to read and understand the Scriptures. One is socio-cultural criticism, a method that investigates the real cultural world in which the biblical texts emerged and grew. What seem to be their values? Why was something a social given or a taboo? Another is narrative criticism, a method that utilizes such techniques as repetition, symmetry, *inclusio* (key words or phrases that begin and end a section), irony, conflict, resolution, and character development. These devices help the reader appreciate the literary artistry of biblical texts. One intention of such criticism is to help the reader understand the text in its own terms (a task of exegesis) and then find meaningful applications for the present (a task of hermeneutics). This commentary will utilize these methods among others.

Great themes and motifs in Leviticus

The literary artistry of Leviticus raises themes and motifs deserving mention as an orientation to this commentary. First, holiness is the primary theme in the book. The intrinsic characteristic of God is being holy (Hebrew *qādôsh*). Holiness in the Scriptures denotes being somehow set apart by nature or by vocation. Thus a priest is set apart by vocation to serve liturgically in holiness and consecration: "You are consecrated to the LORD, and the vessels are also consecrated" (Ezra 8:28). God is holy and sinful humanity seeks holiness.

This perspective leads to a second theme in Leviticus, i.e., the divine presence among the people. How can the all holy God be present to a sinful people? God does not compromise intrinsic holiness in order to engage with creation, and creation is good from the beginning (Gen 1). Humans must grow in holiness to meet the God they love and worship. Leviticus addresses this theological issue throughout. Although the book has a complex history of development toward its final canonical form, the message is clear. Humans strive to grow in holiness but are hindered in that progress by falling into error and sin, both unintentional and intentional. Unintentional errors call for purification; intentional sin demands atonement.

The book also delimits boundaries of cleanness and uncleanness. The issue is not about compliance or non-compliance to dry, constricting laws but about growing in holiness, wholeness, and sincerity before God. Further, Leviticus is not simply about attaining holiness before God in a totally personal relationship. Holiness also bespeaks a holy and wholesome relationship with family and neighbor.

Leviticus 19 introduces in the Scriptures what we call the Golden Rule: love your neighbor as yourself (v. 18). This chapter also mandates care for the poor by leaving a portion of one's crops behind at harvest time (vv. 9-10), and honesty in keeping with the Ten Commandments (vv. 11-12). Rules of sexual conduct serve to maintain integrity in the family and social harmony in the community. Blood and its shedding are closely regulated because life is in the blood (17:11). All the sacrifices, holy days, dietary laws, rules of sexual relations and other bodily contacts, and charity to the poor serve to draw one closer to God. All these instructions are rooted in God's covenant as human obligation: "These are the commandments which the LORD gave Moses on Mount Sinai for the Israelites" (27:34). This intentionality colors all that we read in Leviticus.

Finally, a former Old Testament professor of mine once quipped that in a commentary we read what struck the author's fancy as he/she moved along. That remark came to my mind as I began to research and write this commentary. I hope to highlight what strikes my fancy without becoming fanciful. My goal is that this commentary will offer the popular audience a reading that helps make sense of the book of Leviticus in itself and offer associations for contemporary faith. In sum, the Scriptures are the *Living Word*, and Leviticus still speaks to that lived tradition, both oral and written.

The Book of Leviticus

I. Ritual of Sacrifices

A. Instructions for the Israelites

1 **Burnt Offerings.** [1]The LORD called Moses, and spoke to him from the tent of meeting: [2]Speak to the Israelites and tell them: When any one of you brings an offering of livestock to the LORD, you shall bring your offering from the herd or from the flock.

SACRIFICES AND OFFERINGS

Leviticus 1–7

Leviticus 1–7 covers a variety of sacrifices and offerings. The chapters also introduce holiness/sacredness (Hebrew *qādôsh*, literally, to be set apart; 6:9, 19, 22; 7:6), an important theme that runs through the book. The narrative may be subdivided into two basic sections. Chapters 1–5 relate to sacrifices of the Israelites in general, while chapters 6–7 relate first to sacrifices of the priests and then flows back to the Israelites in general. This sequence creates an "a: b: a" pattern (people: priests: people) in the narrative, centering on the activity of the priests. This narrative technique highlights the central role of the priest as presider and cultic mediator for the priestly nation of Israel.

Chapters 1–5 repeat the phrase "If/when . . ." and then moves to the specific sacrifice involved (1:3, 10, 14; 2:1, 4, 14; 3:1, 6, 12 and so on). The four sacrifices are as follows: burnt offerings, grain offerings, communion sacrifices, and purification offerings. Chapters 6–7 are punctuated by the phrase "This is the ritual . . ." for the priests (6:2, 7, 18; 7:1, 11 and so on) and "Tell the Israelites . . ." (7:22, 29) for the people in general. Such narrative techniques give some order and symmetry to the book.

Moses is the central figure and mediator *par excellence*, harking back to his characterization in Exodus 3–5 and anticipating his role in Numbers and Deuteronomy. That Moses is called and then commanded to speak to the people (Lev 1:1) reflects his biblical characterization as prophet and spokesperson for

11

³If a person's offering is a burnt offering from the herd, the offering must be a male without blemish. The individual shall bring it to the entrance of the tent of meeting to find favor with the LORD, ⁴and shall lay a hand on the head of the burnt offering, so that it may be acceptable to make atonement for the one who offers it. ⁵The bull shall then be slaughtered before the LORD, and Aaron's sons, the priests, shall offer its blood by splashing it on all the sides of the altar which is at the entrance of the tent of meeting. ⁶Then the burnt offering shall be flayed and cut into pieces. ⁷After Aaron's sons, the priests, have put burning embers on the altar and laid wood on them, ⁸they shall lay the pieces of meat, together with the head and the suet, on top of the wood and the embers on the altar; ⁹but the inner organs and the shanks shall be washed with water. The priest shall then burn all of it on the altar as a burnt offering, a sweet-smelling oblation to the LORD.

¹⁰If a person's burnt offering is from the flock, that is, a sheep or a goat, the offering must be a male without blemish. ¹¹It shall be slaughtered on the north side of the altar before the LORD, and Aaron's sons, the priests, shall splash its blood on all the sides of the altar. ¹²When it has been cut into pieces, the priest shall lay these, together with the head and suet, on top of the wood and the embers on the altar; ¹³but the inner organs and the shanks shall be washed with water. The priest shall then offer

---

God in word and deed. Moses is called at the burning bush and sent to speak the Lord's message to Pharaoh: "Let my people go . . ." (Exod 5:1). At first Moses is a reluctant leader: "Who am I that I should go to Pharaoh and bring the Israelites out of Egypt?" (Exod 3:11; cf. 3:13; 4:1, 10, 13). Later he comes into his own and assures the frightened Israelites as they head toward the Red Sea (Exod 14:10-14). In the book of Leviticus Moses addresses the people in a lengthy discourse wherein he shows his character as a decisive leader with privileged access to the Lord. He is the valid and authoritative lawgiver.

1:3-17 Burnt offerings

The sacrifice of a domesticated herd animal (cattle, sheep, or goat) was the primary food offering to gods in the ancient world. The sweet-smelling oblation (vv. 9, 13, 17; cf. Gen 4:1-5; 8:20-22) was voluntary for the most part, motivated by such occasions as a vow, an annual festival, or purification rite. Immolation of the entire animal, apart from the hide, gave full recognition and glory to the Lord. The laying on of a hand (Lev 1:4) was not so much about transferring the sins of the offerer to the animal (cf. 16:20-28, the scapegoat) but affirming the identity of the owner and that person's benefit from the sacrifice. The offerer received a benefit or atonement for making the sacrifice.

all of it, burning it on the altar. It is a burnt offering, a sweet-smelling oblation to the LORD.

¹⁴If a person offers a bird as a burnt offering to the LORD, the offering brought must be a turtledove or a pigeon. ¹⁵Having brought it to the altar, the priest shall wring its head off and burn it on the altar. The blood shall be drained out against the side of the altar. ¹⁶He shall remove its crissum by means of its feathers and throw it on the ash heap at the east side of the altar. ¹⁷Then, having torn the bird open by its wings without separating the halves, the priest shall burn it on the altar, on the wood and the embers. It is a burnt offering, a sweet-smelling oblation to the LORD.

The categories of suitable animals are cited in their descending value. The first category is the male bovine (Hebrew *bāqār*: variously the ox, bull, or calf). In the ancient world only the wealthy could own large herds of bovines. The animal must be without blemish, i.e., not blind, crippled, or maimed; not with running sores, mange, or ringworm (22:22-24). The priest is also prohibited from physical defect (21:17-21).

The second category is the male ovine (sheep, goat), the most common domesticated animal in the ancient world. Their hair, milk (and milk products), skin, meat, bones, and horns were useful to humans. Goats can produce milk even in arid climates, making them useful to nomadic peoples. Like the bovine offering, the ovine must be without blemish.

The third category is the bird (Hebrew *ʿôph*), specified as a turtledove or pigeon. This offering is basically a substitution offering available to the poor (see 5:7; cf. Luke 2:24 [presentation of Jesus]). The text makes no mention of the bird being without blemish. This detail may stem from the fact that a feathered animal would not exhibit blemishes as easily as on a bull, sheep, or goat. The seasonal molting of feathers may have been another case.

The role of blood in the burnt offering deserves comment. Blood is an essential element of sacrifice; it is either sprinkled or squeezed on the altar. Blood joins the human and the divine in a sacred moment. People share in God's holiness through sprinkling of blood. The Day of Atonement highlights the ritual use of blood (16:14-19) and is related theologically to the Israelite covenant at Sinai sealed by blood (cf. Exod 24:3-8). On that occasion Moses sprinkled the holy blood on the people, saying, "This is the blood of the covenant which the LORD has made with you according to all these words" (v. 8).

Chapter 1 sets the tone for the book of Leviticus. First, a relationship with God demands sacred moments of encounter. Liturgy provides such occasions. Second, sacred moments demand a precise order of worship.

2 Grain Offerings. [1]When anyone brings a grain offering to the LORD, the offering must consist of bran flour. The offerer shall pour oil on it and put frankincense over it, [2]and bring it to Aaron's sons, the priests. A priest shall take a handful of the bran flour and oil, together with all the frankincense, and shall burn it on the altar as a token of the offering, a sweet-smelling oblation to the LORD. [3]The rest of the grain offering belongs to Aaron and his sons, a most holy portion from the oblations to the LORD.

[4]When you offer a grain offering baked in an oven, it must be in the form of unleavened cakes made of bran flour mixed with oil, or of unleavened wafers spread with oil. [5]If your offering is a grain offering that is fried on a griddle, it must be of bran flour mixed with oil and unleavened. [6]Break it into pieces, and pour oil over it. It is a grain offering. [7]If your offering is a grain offering that is prepared in a pan, it must be made of bran flour, fried in oil. [8]A grain offering that is made in any of these ways you shall bring to the LORD. It shall be pre-sented to the priest, who shall take it to the altar. [9]The priest shall then remove from the grain offering a token and burn it on the altar as a sweet-smelling obla-tion to the LORD. [10]The rest of the grain offering belongs to Aaron and his sons, a most holy portion from the oblations to the LORD.

[11]Every grain offering that you present to the LORD shall be unleavened, for you shall not burn any leaven or honey as an oblation to the LORD. [12]Such you may present to the LORD in the offering of the first produce that is processed, but they are not to be placed on the altar for a pleasing odor. [13]You shall season all your grain offerings with salt. Do not let the salt of the covenant with your God be lacking from your grain offering. On every offering you shall offer salt.

[14]If you offer a grain offering of first ripe fruits to the LORD, you shall offer it in the form of fresh early grain, roasted by fire and crushed as a grain offering of your first ripe fruits. [15]You shall put oil on it and set frankincense on it. It is a grain offering. [16]The priest shall then

---

The ancients valued ritual integrity as much as moderns do: Who presides? What vestments are worn? What are the proper gifts? What benefit comes from this practice? Third, the gifts brought to worship flow from God's fruits of creation as animal or grain (Gen 1:1–2:4 [P creation account]; 4:1-16 [Cain and Abel]). Fourth, gifts offered to God include some human benefit in return. The subsequent chapters may seem repetitive at times, but the repetition drives home the important lessons of Leviticus. Repetition aids stories rooted in oral tradition, such as much of biblical literature.

2:1-16 Grain offerings

Like the bird offering, the grain offerings are available to the poor. Sev-eral recipes were acceptable, and any offerings mixed with frankincense were burned and not eaten.

burn some of the groats and oil, together with all the frankincense, as a token of the offering, an oblation to the LORD.

3 Communion Sacrifices. ¹If a person's offering is a communion sacrifice, if it is brought from the herd, be it a male or a female animal, it must be presented without blemish before the LORD. ²The one offering it shall lay a hand on the head of the offering. It shall then be slaughtered at the entrance of the tent of meeting. Aaron's sons, the priests, shall splash its blood on all the sides of the altar. ³From the communion sacrifice the individual shall offer as an oblation to the LORD the fat that covers the inner organs, and all the fat that adheres to them, ⁴as well as the two kidneys, with the fat on them near the loins, and the lobe of the liver, which is removed with the kidneys. ⁵Aaron's sons shall burn this on the altar with the burnt offering that is on the wood and the embers, as a sweet-smelling oblation to the LORD.

⁶If the communion sacrifice one offers to the LORD is from the flock, be it a male or a female animal, it must be presented without blemish. ⁷If one presents

---

Frankincense is a large succulent with aromatic sap. Many ancient civilizations imported its expensive gum for ritual use. Its reputed medicinal value was acclaimed in the ancient world. A portion of a cooked offering without frankincense went to the priests as a gift (v. 10). The reasons for the prohibition of leaven or honey remain obscure. Leavened bread was an acceptable thanksgiving offering but never a burnt offering. It may be that these ingredients put off a displeasing smoke and odor unbefitting of a sweet-smelling oblation.

Salt, however, is required of all cereal offerings. Salt was considered a necessity of life and used as a condiment, preservative, and healing agent. It was also a symbol of covenant alliance and friendship as attested here and elsewhere in the Old Testament (Num 18:19 ["covenant of salt"]; 2 Chr 13:5; cf. Mark 9:49-50; Col 4:6).

3:1-17 Communion sacrifices

The essence of peace (Hebrew *shālôm*) is well-being in every aspect of life. The communion sacrifice (also called a peace offering) affirms the harmony and right relation with God and others in the community. Like the burnt offering this offering demands an unblemished bovine or ovine. Selected portions were offered to God, the priest, and the offerer. In practice this offering provided blessed meat for special occasions, since meat was not a daily staple in the ancient world. As with the burnt offerings, blood is splashed on the altar. The occasion for the sacrifice could be thanksgiving for a divine favor, one's completion of a vow, or simply out of generosity. The joyful nature of this offering sets it apart (see 7:11-21).

15

a lamb as an offering, that person shall bring it before the LORD, [8]and after laying a hand on the head of the offering, it shall then be slaughtered before the tent of meeting. Aaron's sons shall splash its blood on all the sides of the altar. [9]From the communion sacrifice the individual shall present as an oblation to the LORD its fat: the whole fatty tail, which is removed close to the spine, the fat that covers the inner organs, and all the fat that adheres to them, [10]as well as the two kidneys, with the fat on them near the loins, and the lobe of the liver, which is removed with the kidneys. [11]The priest shall burn this on the altar as food, an oblation to the LORD.

[12]If a person's offering is a goat, the individual shall bring it before the LORD, [13]and after laying a hand on its head, it shall then be slaughtered before the tent of meeting. Aaron's sons shall splash its blood on all the sides of the altar. [14]From this the one sacrificing shall present an offering as an oblation to the LORD: the fat that covers the inner organs, and all the fat that adheres to them, [15]as well as the two kidneys, with the fat on them near the loins, and the lobe of the liver, which is removed with the kidneys. [16]The priest shall burn these on the altar as food, a sweet-smelling oblation.

All the fat belongs to the LORD. [17]This shall be a perpetual ordinance for your descendants wherever they may dwell. You shall not eat any fat or any blood.

4 Purification Offerings. [1]The LORD said to Moses: [2]Tell the Israelites: When a person inadvertently does wrong by violating any one of the LORD's prohibitions—

One can see that chapters 1–3 present a variety of sacrifices that include sensitivity to the poor in the community. The various rubrics bespeak not mechanical actions that coerce things from God, but a relationship involving right order, often including the laying on of the hand and each person assuming a specific role in the ceremony. The gifts are not random but appropriate to the occasion and offered with care.

The opening chapters of Leviticus show the importance of offerings occasioned out of free will and not just need. The reader may too readily associate Old Testament sacrifice with placating God or atoning for sin. Although atonement informs many sacrifices, the foundation of worship is the covenant. Covenant includes God's commitment to the good creation (Gen 9:1-17 [Noah]; Gen 15 and 17 [Abraham]; 2 Sam 7 [David]) and the human obligation to live as God's people (Exod 24 [Moses]; Josh 24:16-28). Covenant is a two-sided coin in the Scriptures. It offers God's free commitment and, in turn, the human obligation to live by God's laws.

4:1-12 Purification offerings for priests

The occasional designation "sin" offering is misleading. More recent studies distinguish between unintentional ritual impurity and intentional

For the Anointed Priest. ³If it is the anointed priest who thus does wrong and thereby makes the people guilty, he shall offer to the LORD an unblemished bull of the herd as a purification offering for the wrong he committed. ⁴Bringing the bull to the entrance of the tent of meeting, before the LORD, he shall lay his hand on its head and slaughter it before the LORD. ⁵The anointed priest shall then take some of the bull's blood and bring it into the tent of meeting, ⁶where, dipping his finger in the blood, he shall sprinkle some of it seven times before the LORD, toward the veil of the sanctuary. ⁷The priest shall also put some of the blood on the horns of the altar of fragrant incense which stands before the LORD in the tent of meeting. The rest of the bull's blood he shall pour out at the base of the altar for burnt offerings which is at the entrance of the tent of meeting. ⁸He shall remove all the fat of the bull of the purification offering: the fat that covers the inner organs, and all the fat that adheres to them, ⁹as well as the two kidneys, with the fat on them near the loins, and the lobe of the liver, which is removed with the kidneys, ¹⁰just as the fat pieces are removed from the ox of the communion sacrifice. The priest shall burn these on the altar for burnt offerings. ¹¹But the hide of the bull and its meat, with its head, shanks, inner organs and dung, ¹²that is, the whole bull, shall be brought outside the camp to a clean place where the ashes are deposited and there be burned in a wood fire. At the place of the ash heap, there it must be burned.

---

wrongdoing, both of which may demand a sacrifice. This distinction highlights that not all these offerings relate to sin. Some relate to normal bodily functions (menstruation, childbirth), personal ignorance of the law, or acting out of necessity (burial of the dead). Certain actions may make a person *ritually* impure but not all of them are sinful.

The first purification offering belongs to the priests serving in the sanctuary and thus bound to exemplary holiness. This offering involves the threefold sprinkling or pouring of blood. "Horns" of the altar are mentioned for the first time in Leviticus (v. 7). These ornaments projected from the four corners of the altar and probably represented the strength and abiding presence of God, drawing on the mythical qualities of the bull. Cutting off the horns of the altar was an act of desecration (Amos 3:14). The horns are also cited as a place of refuge for transgressors (e.g., 1 Kgs 1:50; 2:28).

Particular attention is given to the fatty parts of the animal, which along with blood were the best gifts. Fat offered in sacrifice must not be consumed by humans (see 3:17; 7:23-25) and blood can never be consumed. Non-sacrificial fat may be eaten. The entire animal is burned outside the camp and its ashes deposited there. The ashes symbolize the reality and efficacy of the purification (cf. Num 19 [ashes of the red heifer]; Heb 9:13).

For the Community. ¹³If the whole community of Israel errs inadvertently and without even being aware of it violates any of the LORD's prohibitions, and thus are guilty, ¹⁴when the wrong that was committed becomes known, the community shall offer a bull of the herd as a purification offering. They shall bring it before the tent of meeting. ¹⁵The elders of the community shall lay their hands on the bull's head before the LORD. When the bull has been slaughtered before the LORD, ¹⁶the anointed priest shall bring some of its blood into the tent of meeting, ¹⁷and dipping his finger in the blood, he shall sprinkle it seven times before the LORD, toward the veil. ¹⁸He shall also put some of the blood on the horns of the altar which is before the LORD in the tent of meeting. The rest of the blood he shall pour out at the base of the altar for burnt offerings which is at the entrance of the tent of meeting. ¹⁹He shall remove all of its fat and burn it on the altar, ²⁰doing with this bull just as he did with the other bull of the purification offering; he will do the same thing. Thus the priest shall make atonement on their behalf, that they may be forgiven. ²¹This bull shall also be brought outside the camp and burned, just as the first bull. It is a purification offering for the assembly.

For the Tribal Leader. ²²Should a tribal leader do wrong inadvertently by violating any one of the prohibitions of the LORD his God, and thus be guilty, ²³when he learns of the wrong he committed, he shall bring as his offering an unblemished male goat. ²⁴He shall lay his hand on its head and it shall be slaughtered in the place where the burnt offering is slaughtered, before the LORD. It is a purification offering. ²⁵The priest shall then take some of the blood of the purification offering on his finger and put it on the horns of the altar for burnt offerings. The rest of the blood he shall pour out at the base of the altar. ²⁶All of its fat he shall burn on the altar like the

---

4:13-21 Purification for the community

The whole community includes the priests and the people. This sacrifice closely mirrors the purification offering of the priest discussed above. However, on this occasion the community, not the priest, brings the bull forward (v. 14). The exact nature of this assembly remains obscure. Has the entire community sinned, or the community leaders who corporately represent them all? Whichever the case, this sacrifice acknowledges the reality of communal need for atonement. Offering a bull purifies the sanctuary and brings the community back into a right relationship with God. The greatest time of purification is the Day of Atonement discussed later in Leviticus.

4:22-26 Purification for the tribal leaders

The tribal leader (Hebrew *nāśîʾ*, literally, "one raised up") comprises a variety of officials in ancient Israel. For example, the term can designate

The Wailing Wall, Jerusalem

fat of the communion sacrifice. Thus the priest shall make atonement on the tribal leader's behalf for his wrong, that he may be forgiven.

For the General Populace. [27]If anyone of the general populace does wrong inadvertently by violating one of the LORD's prohibitions, and thus is guilty, [28]upon learning of the wrong committed, that person shall bring an unblemished she-goat as the offering for the wrong committed. [29]The wrongdoer shall lay a hand on the head of the purification offering, and the purification offering shall be slaughtered at the place of the burnt offerings. [30]The priest shall then take some of its blood on his finger and put it on the horns of the altar for burnt offerings. The rest of the blood he shall pour out at the base of the altar. [31]He shall remove all the fat, just as the fat is removed from the communion sacrifice. The priest shall burn it on the altar for a sweet odor to the LORD. Thus the priest shall make atonement, so that the individual may be forgiven.

[32]If, however, a person brings a lamb as a purification offering, that person shall bring an unblemished female, and [33]lay a hand on its head. It shall be slaughtered as a purification offering in the place where the burnt offering is slaughtered. [34]The priest shall then take some of the blood of the purification offering on his finger and put it on the horns of the altar for burnt offerings. The rest of the blood he shall pour out at the base of the altar. [35]He shall remove all its fat just as the fat is removed from the lamb of the communion sacrifice. The priest shall burn these on the altar with the other oblations for the LORD. Thus the priest shall make atonement on the person's behalf for the wrong committed, that the individual may be forgiven.

---

the head of a small group or a tribe. Since he is a leader of the community, the sin of a tribal leader has broader impact. He is called to a higher level of accountability, but his subordination to the priests is reflected in the fact that a goat suffices as an offering. One can see that the value of a sacrificial animal sometimes reflects the status of the offerer and not just one's wealth.

4:27-35 For the general populace

The so-called private person (of the general populace) is literally an individual from among "the people of the land" (Hebrew *ʾam hāʾāres*). The designation "people of the land" has several meanings in the Scriptures, depending on the historical period or context involved. It can mean citizens in good standing (excluding foreigners and slaves), the powerful elite, or even lower classes. In this account such persons are citizens enfranchised with rights and responsibilities representative of their status in society. They may bring a goat or lamb of sacrifice. The option of a bird or grain purification offering by the poor is discussed in chapter 5.

5 Special Cases for Purification Offerings. [1]If a person, either having seen or come to know something, does wrong by refusing as a witness under oath to give information, that individual shall bear the penalty; [2]or if someone, without being aware of it, touches any unclean thing, such as the carcass of an unclean wild animal, or an unclean domestic animal, or an unclean swarming creature, and thus is unclean and guilty; [3]or if someone, without being aware of it, touches some human uncleanness, whatever kind of uncleanness this may be, and then subsequently becomes aware of guilt; [4]or if someone, without being aware of it, rashly utters an oath with bad or good intent, whatever kind of oath this may be, and then subsequently becomes aware of guilt in regard to any of these matters— [5]when someone is guilty in regard to any of these matters, that person shall confess the wrong committed, [6]and make reparation to the Lord for the wrong committed: a female animal from the flock, a ewe lamb or a she-goat, as a purification offering. Thus the priest shall make atonement on the individual's behalf for the wrong.

[7]If, however, the person cannot afford an animal of the flock, that person shall bring to the Lord as reparation for the wrong committed two turtledoves or two pigeons, one for a purification offering and the other for a burnt offering. [8]The guilty party shall bring them to the priest, who shall offer the one for the purification offering first. Wringing its head at the neck, yet without breaking it off, [9]he shall sprinkle some of the blood of the purification offering against the side of the altar. The rest of the blood shall be drained out against the base of the altar. It is a purification offering. [10]The other bird he shall offer as a burnt offering according to procedure. Thus the priest shall make atonement on the person's behalf for the wrong committed, so that the individual may be forgiven.

[11]If the person is unable to afford even two turtledoves or two pigeons, that person shall bring as an offering for the wrong committed one tenth of an ephah of bran flour for a purification offering. The guilty party shall not put oil or place

---

5:1-13 For special cases

Attention to special cases shows that Leviticus wants to be as thorough as possible about purification and atonement. Several representative examples are cited: failure to give legal testimony (v. 1), touching an unclean animal or person (vv. 2-3), and making a rash oath (v. 4). These laws take economic hardship into consideration, a theme that began in chapter 1 and is highlighted in this chapter by the twofold repetition of the phrase "If, however, the person cannot afford . . ." (vv. 7, 11). The appropriate sacrifice in such instances is a female ovine, a bird, or a cereal offering.

It is noteworthy that special cases are not all about economic hardship. Poverty is no excuse for not making eventual atonement. Responsibility demands performing the required ritual even if realized well after the fact.

frankincense on it, because it is a purification offering. [12]The individual shall bring it to the priest, who shall take a handful as a token of the offering and burn it on the altar with the other oblations for the Lord. It is a purification offering. [13]Thus the priest shall make atonement on the person's behalf for the wrong committed in any of the above cases, so that the individual may be forgiven. The rest of the offering, like the grain offering, shall belong to the priest.

Reparation Offerings. [14]The Lord said to Moses: [15]When a person commits sacrilege by inadvertently misusing any of the Lord's sacred objects, the wrongdoer shall bring to the Lord as reparation an unblemished ram from the flock, at the established value in silver shekels according to the sanctuary shekel, as a reparation offering. [16]The wrongdoer shall also restore what has been misused of the sacred objects, adding a fifth of its value, and give this to the priest. Thus the priest shall make atonement for the person with the ram of the reparation offering, so that the individual may be forgiven.

[17]If someone does wrong and violates one of the Lord's prohibitions without realizing it, that person is guilty and shall bear the penalty. [18]The individual shall bring to the priest an unblemished ram of the flock, at the established value, for a reparation offering. The priest shall then make atonement on the offerer's behalf for the error inadvertently and unknowingly committed so that the individual may be forgiven. [19]It is a reparation offering. The individual must make reparation to the Lord.

[20]The Lord said to Moses: [21]When someone does wrong and commits sacrilege against the Lord by deceiving a neighbor about a deposit or a pledge or a stolen article, or by otherwise retaining a neighbor's goods unjustly; [22]or if, having found a lost article, the person lies about it, swearing falsely about any of the things that a person may do wrong— [23]when someone has thus done wrong and is guilty, that person shall restore the thing that was stolen, the item unjustly retained, the item left as deposit, or the lost article that was found [24]or whatever else the individual swore falsely about. That person shall make full restitution of the thing itself, and add one fifth of its value to it, giving it to its owner at the time of reparation. [25]Then that person shall bring to

---

5:14-26 Reparation offerings

This offering, sometimes called a guilt offering, includes occasions of intentional and unintentional impurity. The first case is the unintended act of cheating in sacrificial dues (v. 17). An unblemished ram of a certain monetary value suffices for atonement. The exact worth of a sanctuary shekel remains uncertain because coinage was valued by weight and not by face value. The second case relates to the first, citing instances of an unintentional breaking of a commandment. The third case relates to intentional dishonesty and is discussed in greater detail (seven verses, the length of the previous two cases combined).

the priest as reparation to the Lord an unblemished ram of the flock, at the established value, as a reparation offering. ²⁶The priest shall make atonement on the person's behalf before the Lord, so that the individual may be forgiven for whatever was done to incur guilt.

B. Instructions for the Priests

6 The Daily Burnt Offering. ¹The Lord said to Moses: ²Give Aaron and his sons the following command: This is the ritual for the burnt offering—the burnt offering that is to remain on the hearth of the altar all night until the next morning, while the fire is kept burning on the altar. ³The priest, clothed in his linen robe and wearing linen pants underneath, shall take away the ashes to which the fire has reduced the burnt offering on the altar, and lay them at the side of the altar. ⁴Then, having taken off these garments and put on other garments, he shall carry the ashes to a clean place outside the camp. ⁵The fire on the altar is to be kept burning; it must not go out. Every morning the priest shall put firewood on it. On this he shall lay out the burnt offering and burn the fat of the communion offering. ⁶The fire is to be kept burning continuously on the altar; it must not go out.

The Grain Offering. ⁷This is the ritual of the grain offering. Aaron's sons shall offer it before the Lord, in front of

---

The various offerings in chapters 4 and 5 distinguish between inadvertent and intentional wrongdoing. Both occasions demand reparation and restitution. It would be "cheap grace" for a person to atone via a simple offering and not compensate the person wronged. The prophets railed against sacrifices driven by formalities but without the proper interior disposition. Legal justice demands moral justice as well.

6:1-6 The daily burnt offering

Chapters 6–7 discuss instructions for the priests regarding the various offerings. The narrative is punctuated by the phrase "This is the ritual . . ." (Hebrew *tôrâ* or *tôrat*, literally, "instruction," 6:2, 7, 18; 7:1, 11, 37). The commands are enjoined on Aaron and his sons, a designation for a class of priests more than succession by bloodline. Aaron and his sons are the only priests who preside at rituals in Leviticus. The ordination of the Aaronide class is discussed in chapters 8–9.

The whole burnt offering comes from the verb meaning "to go up" (Hebrew *ʿôlâ*). The offering ascends to the Lord as a fragrant offering with spatial and visual symbolism. Attention is given to the priest's vestments for this sacrifice. The linen robe and drawers represent fine fabric befitting the priest (Exod 28:4-5). Linen, usually bleached to shades of white, was cool to wear in hot and humid weather. Removal of ashes occurs in two stages: to the side of the altar and then outside the camp. The altar is sacred

the altar. ⁸A priest shall then take from the grain offering a handful of bran flour and oil, together with all the frankincense that is on it, and this he shall burn on the altar as a token of the offering, a sweet aroma to the LORD. ⁹The rest of it Aaron and his sons may eat; but it must be eaten unleavened in a sacred place: in the court of the tent of meeting they shall eat it. ¹⁰It shall not be baked with leaven. I have given it to them as their portion from the oblations for the LORD; it is most holy, like the purification offering and the reparation offering. ¹¹Every male of Aaron's descendants may eat of it perpetually throughout your generations as their rightful due from the oblations for the LORD. Whatever touches the oblations becomes holy.

High Priest's Daily Grain Offering. ¹²The LORD said to Moses: ¹³This is the offering that Aaron and his sons shall present to the LORD on the day he is anointed: one tenth of an ephah of bran flour for the regular grain offering, half of it in the morning and half of it in the evening. ¹⁴You shall bring it well kneaded and fried in oil on a griddle. Having broken the offering into pieces, you shall present it as a sweet aroma to the LORD. ¹⁵The anointed priest descended from Aaron who succeeds him shall do likewise. This is the LORD's due forever. The offering shall be wholly burned. ¹⁶Every grain offering of a priest shall be a whole offering; it may not be eaten.

Purification Offerings. ¹⁷The LORD said to Moses: ¹⁸Tell Aaron and his sons:

---

as the place of divine presence and a traditional place of covenant-making. The priest dresses appropriately and makes a change of clothes during the removal. This re-vesting respects the distinction between the holy sanctuary and all space outside of it.

The continuous fire on the altar also highlights the holiness of the sanctuary. Maintaining the fire is an obvious convenience, but it also offers a point of continuity between sacrifices and a vigilant respect for God's abiding presence even when people are absent. A modern parallel would be the perpetual sanctuary lamp in some Christian churches.

6:7-16 Daily grain offering

This offering of the priest actually comprises two separate laws (vv. 7-11 and 12-16) and takes up the discussion of the grain offering in chapter 2. The first law highlights the priest eating the offering in a sacred place, i.e., the court of the meeting tent. The second law demands that the grain be a whole burnt offering to God. These daily sacrifices are cited in Hebrews 7:27 to explain how the perfect sacrifice of Jesus the high priest is once and for all.

6:17-23 Purification offerings

This offering, first mentioned in chapter 4, highlights which offerings the priest may consume, as well as his sacred duties in the slaughter of burnt of-

This is the ritual for the purification offering. At the place where the burnt offering is slaughtered, there also, before the LORD, shall the purification offering be slaughtered. It is most holy. ¹⁹The priest who offers the purification offering shall eat of it; it shall be eaten in a sacred place, in the court of the tent of meeting. ²⁰Whatever touches its flesh becomes holy. If any of its blood spatters on a garment, the stained part must be washed in a sacred place. ²¹A clay vessel in which it has been boiled shall be broken; if it is boiled in a copper vessel, this shall be scoured afterward and rinsed with water. ²²Every male of the priestly line may eat it. It is most holy. ²³But no purification offering of which some blood has been brought into the tent of meeting to make atonement in the sanc-tuary shall be eaten; it must be burned with fire.

7 Reparation Offerings. ¹This is the ritual for the reparation offering. It is most holy. ²At the place where the burnt offering is slaughtered, the reparation offering shall also be slaughtered. Its blood shall be splashed on all the sides of the altar. ³All of its fat shall be offered: the fatty tail, the fat that covers the inner organs, and all the fat that adheres to them, ⁴as well as the two kidneys with the fat on them near the loins, and the lobe of the liver, which is removed with the kidneys. ⁵The priest shall burn these on the altar as an oblation to the LORD. It is a reparation offering. ⁶Every male of the priestly line may eat of it; but it must be eaten in a sacred place. It is most holy.

ferings. The details here exceed those of previous chapters and reiterate the importance of holiness (v. 20). Holy blood is a powerful element in sacrifice and must be handled with care. Sacred vessels are treated with utmost care because they come into contact with the holy. Both clay and bronze vessels are cited. Earthenware must be broken and metal scoured. Earthenware was probably disposable because of its absorbency and fragility.

Shattering pottery is a vivid symbol of divine punishment in the Old Testament: "Thus will I smash this people and this city, as one smashes a clay pot so that it cannot be repaired" (Jer 19:11; cf. Ps 2:9). Metal vessels are more durable and must be purified before further ritual use. Such details in the narrative bespeak reverence of the sacred and the proper care of liturgical objects. In the New Testament Jesus uses cups, jugs, and kettles to condemn token ritual washing without the proper inner disposition (Mark 7:1-8).

7:1-10 Reparation offerings

This offering, first mentioned in 5:14-26, gives particular attention to the fatty portions offered on the altar. The smoke that fat produces would enhance the visual effect and aroma. One may also present a grain offering.

[7]Because the purification offering and the reparation offering are alike, both have the same ritual. The reparation offering belongs to the priest who makes atonement with it. [8]As for the priest who offers someone's burnt offering, to him belongs the hide of the burnt offering that is offered. [9]Also, every grain offering that is baked in an oven or made in a pan or on a griddle shall belong to the priest who offers it, [10]whereas all grain offerings that are mixed with oil or are dry shall belong to all of Aaron's sons without distinction.

Communion Sacrifices. [11]This is the ritual for the communion sacrifice that is offered to the LORD. [12]If someone offers it for thanksgiving, that person shall offer it with unleavened cakes mixed with oil, unleavened wafers spread with oil, and cakes made of bran flour mixed with oil and well kneaded. [13]One shall present this offering together with loaves of leavened bread along with the thanksgiving communion sacrifice. [14]From this the individual shall offer one bread of each type of offering as a contribution to the LORD; this shall belong to the priest who splashes the blood of the communion offering.

[15]The meat of the thanksgiving communion sacrifice shall be eaten on the day it is offered; none of it may be kept till the next morning. [16]However, if the sacrifice offered is a votive or a voluntary offering, it shall be eaten on the day the sacrifice is offered, and on the next day what is left over may be eaten. [17]But what is left over of the meat of the sacrifice on the third day must be burned in the fire. [18]If indeed any of the flesh of the communion sacrifice is eaten on the third day, it shall not be accepted; it will not be reckoned to the credit of the one offering it. Rather it becomes a desecrated meat. Anyone who eats of it shall bear the penalty.

[19]Should the meat touch anything unclean, it may not be eaten, but shall be

---

The distinction between the grain eaten by one priest or to be shared by all the priests remains obscure. Whatever the reason, laypersons do not partake of this offering.

7:11-21 Communion sacrifices

First mentioned in chapter 3, this ritual has the distinction of being eaten by priests and laity alike. Thanksgiving for release from affliction or prayers answered may occasion such a ritual meal. Particular attention is given to the meal being consumed that day and kept from anyone and anything unclean.

This section introduces the notion of being "cut off" (Hebrew *kārat*, 7:20, 21, 25, 27) from the people, a state that bespeaks excommunication and even death. The emphasis is on divine judgment, for the Lord sees through human cover-up or oversight. Even if the guilty person is acquitted in a human court, God's eventual judgment is certain. The theme of being cut off recurs in chapters 17–20.

burned in the fire. As for other meat, all who are clean may eat of it. ²⁰If, however, someone in a state of uncleanness eats the meat of a communion sacrifice belonging to the LORD, that person shall be cut off from the people. ²¹Likewise, if someone touches anything unclean, whether it be human uncleanness or an unclean animal or an unclean loathsome creature, and then eats the meat of the communion sacrifice belonging to the LORD, that person, too, shall be cut off from the people.

Prohibition Against Blood and Fat. ²²The LORD said to Moses: ²³Tell the Israelites: You shall not eat the fat of any ox or sheep or goat. ²⁴Although the fat of an animal that has died a natural death or has been killed by wild beasts may be put to any other use, you may not eat it. ²⁵If anyone eats the fat of an animal from which an oblation is made to the LORD, that person shall be cut off from the people. ²⁶Wherever you dwell, you shall not eat any blood, whether of bird or of animal. ²⁷Every person who eats any blood shall be cut off from the people.

Portions from the Communion Sacrifice for Priests. ²⁸The LORD said to Moses: ²⁹Tell the Israelites: The person who offers a communion sacrifice to the LORD shall be the one to bring from it the offering to the LORD. ³⁰The offerer's own hands shall carry the oblations for the LORD: the person shall bring the fat together with the brisket, which is to be raised as an elevated offering before the LORD. ³¹The priest shall burn the fat on the altar, but the brisket belongs to Aaron and his sons. ³²Moreover, from your communion sacrifices you shall give to the priest the right leg as a contribution. ³³The one among Aaron's sons who offers the blood and the fat of the communion offering shall have the right leg as his portion, ³⁴for from the communion sacrifices of the Israelites I have taken the brisket that is elevated and the leg that is a contribution, and I have given them to Aaron, the priest, and to his sons as their due from the Israelites forever.

³⁵This is the priestly share from the oblations for the LORD, allotted to Aaron

---

7:22-27 Prohibition against blood and fat

This section highlights the sacredness of *sacrificial* fat and blood of *any* kind, neither of which is to be consumed (3:16-17). These portions are set apart to the Lord as holy. In pagan religions fat was food for the gods, but ancient Israel never embraced the idea that their God was dependent on food (Ps 50:12-14). Fat bespeaks offering the best of what one has, a metaphor that calls to mind the phrase "the fat of the land" (Gen 45:18).

7:28-38 The portions for priests

Certain delicacies from the sacrificial animal go to the priest as a gift. The elevated offering, sometimes called a wave offering, includes upward gestures representing the object being dedicated to God and certain parts blessed for the priest's meal. Such elevation rites are also cited of gold for the tabernacle (Exod 35:22) and new grain at the harvest (Lev 23:15-17).

and his sons on the day they were brought forth to be the priests of the LORD, ³⁶which the LORD ordered to be given them from the Israelites on the day they were anointed, as their due throughout their generations forever.

Summary. ³⁷This is the ritual for the burnt offering, the grain offering, the purification offering, the reparation offering, the ordination offering, and the communion sacrifice, ³⁸which the LORD enjoined on Moses at Mount Sinai at the time when he commanded the Israelites in the wilderness of Sinai to bring their offerings to the LORD.

II. Ceremony of Ordination

Ordination of Aaron and His Sons. ▶
8 ¹The LORD said to Moses: ²Take Aaron along with his sons, the vest-

---

Verses 37-38 close Leviticus 1–7 and introduce the ordination offering. The term for ordination (Hebrew *mālēʾ*, literally, "to be full") suggests the portions of a sacrifice placed in the hands of the priest, as well as his being set apart by divine choice and his hand "filled" with a special duty. This imagery of filled hands bespeaks the privilege and responsibility of the priest.

In sum, Leviticus 1–7 discuss a variety of laws and sacrifices unified by the call to holiness, the value of communal ritual, and the benefits that come from embracing and maintaining right relationship with God. The priests and attendants of the sanctuary must have the proper interior disposition and perform their duties according to proper form. These values flow into the theme of ordination in chapters 8–10. The priest has prestige and responsibilities, but his vocation is fraught with danger as the death of Nadab and Abihu will show.

CEREMONY OF ORDINATION

Leviticus 8–10

Moses presides at the ordination of Aaron and his sons and instructs that priestly line about rules of right conduct (cf. Exod 29). Several points are noteworthy. First, Moses literally bathes and then dresses Aaron in his vestments (8:6-9), an intimate gesture that recalls the Lord dressing Adam and Eve before their banishment from Eden (Gen 3:21) and personally shutting Noah and his remnant in the ark at the great flood (Gen 7:16). Second, the repetition of the phrase "as the LORD had commanded" (8:4, 9, 13, 17, 21, 29; 9:7, 10; 10:15) and similar statements emphasize the valid and licit nature of the rite and create a bold contrast to the disobedience

---

▶ This symbol indicates a cross reference number in the *Catechism of the Catholic Church*. See page 99 for number citations.

ments, the anointing oil, the bull for a purification offering, the two rams, and the basket of unleavened bread, ³then assemble the whole community at the entrance of the tent of meeting. ⁴Moses did as the LORD had commanded. When the community had assembled at the entrance of the tent of meeting, ⁵Moses told them: "This is what the LORD has ordered to be done." ⁶Bringing forward Aaron and his sons, Moses first washed them with water. ⁷Then he put the tunic on Aaron, girded him with the sash, clothed him with the robe, placed the ephod on him, and girded him with the ephod's embroidered belt, fastening the ephod on him with it. ⁸He then set the breastpiece on him, putting the Urim and Thummim in it. ⁹He put the turban on his head, attaching the gold medallion, the sacred headband, on the front of the turban, as the LORD had commanded Moses to do.

¹⁰Taking the anointing oil, Moses anointed and consecrated the tabernacle and all that was in it. ¹¹Then he sprinkled some of the oil seven times on the altar, and anointed the altar, with all its utensils, and the laver, with its base, to consecrate them. ¹²He also poured some of the ▶

---

of Nadab and Abihu (10:1). Third, the themes of summoning, assembling, and bringing forth inform the narrative (8:1-6, 14, 18, 22; 9:1, 5, 8, 15). The liturgical style of these chapters is striking.

The narrative also highlights the mediatory character of Moses as he facilitates the Lord's will for valid ordinations. Moses enjoys such a status because he is a friend of God, a relationship beautifully described in Exodus 33:7-23. Verse 11 is a key statement in that passage: "The LORD used to speak to Moses face to face, as a person speaks to a friend."

The modern reader can better appreciate this section by associating it with lived experience. Life stages bring so-called "rites of passage" to which all can relate in some way: birthdays, receiving sacraments, graduations, becoming parents or grandparents. Ordinations and other calls to ministry characterize modern faith as much as they did for the readers of Leviticus 8–10. Being called, consecrated, instructed in proper service, and embracing moral living remain perpetual values.

8:1-13 Ordination of Aaron and his sons

The items mentioned in verse 2 equip Moses for leading the ceremony. The vestments denote distinctive attire associated with the temple and sacrifice (see Exod 28 and 39 for details about the vestments). The anointing oil is used to consecrate the sacred furnishings and the priests, setting both apart from others (Levites and laypersons). The rams and unleavened bread are gifts for sacrifice. More will be stated below about oil and the sacrificial animals.

anointing oil on Aaron's head and anointed him, to consecrate him. ¹³Moses likewise brought forward Aaron's sons, clothed them with tunics, girded them with sashes, and put skullcaps on them, as the LORD had commanded him to do.

Ordination Sacrifices. ¹⁴He brought forward the bull for a purification offering, and Aaron and his sons laid their hands on its head. ¹⁵When it was slaughtered, Moses took the blood and with his finger he put it on the horns around the altar, thus purifying the altar. He poured out the rest of the blood at the base of the altar. Thus he consecrated it so that atonement could be made on it. ¹⁶Taking all the fat that was over the inner organs, as well as the lobe of the liver and the two kidneys with their fat, Moses burned them on the altar. ¹⁷The bull, however, with its hide and flesh and dung he burned in the fire outside the camp, as the LORD had commanded Moses to do.

¹⁸He next brought forward the ram of the burnt offering, and Aaron and his sons laid their hands on its head. ¹⁹When it was slaughtered, Moses splashed the blood on all sides of the altar. ²⁰After the ram was cut up into pieces, Moses burned the head, the cut-up pieces and the suet. ²¹After the inner organs and the shanks were washed with water, Moses burned these remaining parts of the ram on the altar. It was a burnt offering for a sweet aroma, an oblation to the LORD, as the LORD had commanded Moses.

²²Then he brought forward the second ram, the ordination ram, and Aaron and his sons laid their hands on its head. ²³When it was slaughtered, Moses took some of its blood and put it on the lobe of Aaron's right ear, on the thumb of his right hand, and on the big toe of his right foot. ²⁴Moses had the sons of Aaron also come forward, and he put some of the blood on the lobes of their right ears, on the thumbs of their right hands, and on the big toes of their right feet. The rest of the blood he splashed on all the sides of the altar. ²⁵He then took the fat: the fatty tail and all the fat over the inner organs, the lobe of the liver and the two kidneys with their fat, and likewise the right thigh; ²⁶from the basket of unleavened bread that was set before the LORD he took one unleavened cake, one loaf of bread made with oil, and one wafer; these he placed on top of the portions of fat and the right thigh. ²⁷He then put all these things upon the palms of Aaron and his sons, whom he had raise them as an elevated offering before the LORD. ²⁸When Moses had removed them from their palms, he burned them on the altar with the burnt offering. They were an ordination offering for a sweet aroma, an oblation to the LORD. ²⁹He then took the

---

8:14-36 Ordination sacrifices

This ritual mirrors the account in Exodus 29:10-14. Moses' purifying the altar (v. 15) prepares it for consecrating the many offerings to be laid upon it. The two rams cited in verse 2 are then sacrificed. The first ram, like the bull, is a burnt offering. The second is called the ordination ram (see 7:37). It atones for any sins of Aaron and his sons and dedicates them to the Lord.

brisket and raised it as an elevated offering before the LORD; this was Moses' own portion of the ordination ram, as the LORD had commanded Moses. [30]Taking some of the anointing oil and some of the blood that was on the altar, Moses sprinkled it upon Aaron and his vestments, as well as his sons and their vestments, thus consecrating both Aaron and his vestments and his sons and their vestments.

[31]Moses said to Aaron and his sons, "Boil the meat at the entrance of the tent of meeting, and there eat it with the bread that is in the basket of the ordination offering, in keeping with the command I have received: 'Aaron and his sons shall eat of it.' [32]What is left over of the meat and the bread you shall burn in the fire. [33]Moreover, you are not to depart from the entrance of the tent of meeting for seven days, until the days of your ordination are completed; for your ordination is to last for seven days. [34]What has been done today the LORD has commanded be done, to make atonement for you. [35]You must remain at the entrance of the tent of meeting day and night for seven days, carrying out the prescriptions of the LORD, so that you do not die, for this is the command I have received." [36]So Aaron and his sons did all that the LORD had commanded through Moses.

The details in verses 22-24 highlight the central moment of ordination itself. Blood is daubed on parts of the right side of the body, from upper to lower extremities: ear, thumb, and toe. In ancient societies (and some Middle Eastern countries today), the right hand was "clean" and used to touch another person. Sitting at someone's right hand was the position of honor at banquets and ceremonies (Ps 110:1, 5). The ear, thumb, and toe symbolize, respectively, listening to God's words, having hands pure for leading sacrifices, and walking with God (see Deut 30:16). In every aspect of his life the priest is consecrated by the blood. His whole being belongs to divine service. His dedication calls to mind Psalm 19:15, "Let the words of my mouth be acceptable / the thoughts of my heart before you, / LORD, my rock and my redeemer."

The elevation offering of unleavened food, placed in their hands by Moses, is a gift from Aaron and his sons to the Lord. Reciprocally, their sprinkling with oil and blood from the altar further consecrates the priests and their vestments. After a ritual meal, the newly ordained must stay at the entrance of the meeting tent for seven days, seven being the biblical number of completion, perfection, and wholeness (cf. Gen 2:1-3).

Verse 36 closes the chapter. The newly ordained, Aaron and his sons, now do all the things commanded by the Lord through Moses. Proper authority and protocol have been observed as the many details in the chapter confirm. Chapters 9–10 move from hearing about the proper conduct of the priest to their acting it out in their daily duties.

9 **Octave of the Ordination.** ¹On the eighth day Moses summoned Aaron and his sons, together with the elders of Israel, ²and said to Aaron, "Take a calf of the herd for a purification offering and a ram for a burnt offering, both without blemish, and offer them before the LORD. ³Tell the Israelites, too: Take a he-goat for a purification offering, a calf and a lamb, both unblemished yearlings, for a burnt offering, ⁴and an ox and a ram for a communion sacrifice, to sacrifice before the LORD, along with a grain offering mixed with oil; for today the LORD will appear to you." ⁵So they brought what Moses had ordered before the tent of meeting. When the whole community had come forward and stood before the LORD, ⁶Moses said, "This is what the LORD orders you to do, that the glory of the LORD may appear to you. ⁷Approach the altar," Moses then told Aaron, "and make your purification offering and your burnt offering in atonement for yourself and for your household; then make the offering of the people in atonement for them, as the LORD has commanded."

⁸Approaching the altar, Aaron first slaughtered the calf of the purification offering that was his own offering. ⁹When his sons presented the blood to him, he dipped his finger in the blood and put it on the horns of the altar. The rest of the blood he poured out at the base of the altar. ¹⁰He then burned on the altar the fat, the kidneys and the lobe of the liver from the purification offering, as the LORD had commanded Moses; ¹¹but the flesh and the hide he burned in the fire outside the camp. ¹²Then Aaron slaughtered the burnt offering. When his sons brought him the blood, he splashed it on all sides of the altar. ¹³They then brought him the pieces and the head of the burnt offering, and he burned them on the altar. ¹⁴Having washed the inner organs and the shanks, he burned these also with the burnt offering on the altar.

¹⁵Then he had the people's offering brought. Taking the goat that was for the

---

9:1-24 Octave of the ordination

On the eighth or octave day of ordination, Aaron and his sons officiate at their first sacrifices. The list comprises the variety of offerings enjoined so far: burnt offering, purification, communion, grain, etc. The presence of the Lord confirms the efficacy of their ordination (vv. 4, 6). Divine presence at these ritual moments affirms the great events at Sinai as abiding and now present in the meeting tent. The awesome divine powers of Sinai are demonstrated anew in fire coming forth from the Lord's presence and consuming the burnt offering and remnants of fat on the altar (v. 24). This awesome event anticipated the death of Nadab and Abihu that follows. It also calls to mind Elijah's encounter with the prophets of Baal where fire from heaven consumed his burnt offering: "The LORD's fire came down and devoured the burnt offering, wood, stones, and dust, and lapped up the water in the trench" (1 Kgs 18:38).

people's purification offering, he slaughtered it and offered it as a purification offering as before. ¹⁶Then he brought forward the burnt offering and offered it according to procedure. ¹⁷He then presented the grain offering; taking a handful of it, he burned it on the altar, in addition to the morning burnt offering. ¹⁸Finally he slaughtered the ox and the ram, the communion sacrifice of the people. When his sons brought him the blood, Aaron splashed it on all sides of the altar. ¹⁹The portions of fat from the ox and from the ram, the fatty tail, the covering fat, the kidneys, and the lobe of the liver ²⁰they placed on top of the briskets. Aaron burned the fat pieces on the altar, ²¹but the briskets and the right thigh he raised as an elevated offering before the LORD, as the LORD had commanded Moses.

Revelation of the Lord's Glory. ²²Aaron then raised his hands over the people and blessed them. When he came down from offering the purification offering, the burnt offering, and the communion offering, ²³Moses and Aaron went into the tent of meeting. On coming out they blessed the people. Then the glory of the LORD appeared to all the people. ²⁴Fire came forth from the LORD's presence and consumed the burnt offering and the fat on the altar. Seeing this, all the people shouted with joy and fell prostrate.

10 Nadab and Abihu. ¹Aaron's sons Nadab and Abihu took their censers and, putting incense on the fire they

---

Verses 22-24 create a fitting climax to the chapter. With preparations ready and sacrifices offered, Aaron raises his hands in blessing. Though his words of blessing are not quoted, the blessing of Aaron in Numbers 6:24-26 would be a fitting selection: "The LORD bless you and keep you! / The LORD let his face shine upon you, and be gracious to you! / The LORD look upon you kindly and give you peace!"

Now for the first time Moses and Aaron enter the tent of meeting. The elaborate preparations lead to this climactic moment. It is noteworthy that the phrase "all the people" is stated twice at the end (vv. 23-24). This sacred moment is not just about Moses, priests, and attendants in their realm of the sacred. The presence and response of the Israelites is also essential. God's glory is revealed to all present. Finally, the theme of obedience punctuates this chapter. Such repetitions as "then he/they brought . . ." (vv. 5, 12-13, 16, 18) show the order and careful execution of every step. The priests must not forget what they have been taught lest they receive the fate of Nadab and Abihu.

10:1-5 Nadab and Abihu

This tragic episode is triggered by the offering of an unauthorized fire (Hebrew ʾēsh zārâ, literally, "alien fire"). The exact nature of the offense

had set in them, they offered before the LORD unauthorized fire, such as he had not commanded. [2]Fire therefore came forth from the LORD's presence and consumed them, so that they died in the LORD's presence. [3]Moses then said to Aaron, "This is as the LORD said:

Through those near to me I will be sanctified;
in the sight of all the people I will obtain glory."

But Aaron said nothing. [4]Then Moses summoned Mishael and Elzaphan, the sons of Aaron's uncle Uzziel, with the order, "Come, carry your kinsmen from before the sanctuary to a place outside the camp." [5]So they drew near and carried them by means of their tunics outside the camp, as Moses had commanded.

Conduct of the Priests. [6]Moses said to Aaron and his sons Eleazar and Ithamar, "Do not dishevel your hair or tear your garments, lest you die and bring God's wrath also on the whole community. While your kindred, the rest of the house of Israel, may mourn for those whom the LORD's fire has burned up, [7]you shall not go beyond the entrance of the tent of meeting, else you shall die; for the anointing oil of the LORD is upon you." So they did as Moses told them.

[8]The LORD said to Aaron: [9]When you are to go to the tent of meeting, you and your sons are forbidden, by a perpetual statute throughout your generations, to drink any wine or strong drink, lest you die. [10]You must be able to distinguish between what is sacred and what is profane, and between what is clean and what is unclean; [11]and you must be able to teach the Israelites all the statutes that the LORD has given them through Moses.

The Eating of the Priestly Portions. [12]Moses said to Aaron and his surviving sons, Eleazar and Ithamar, "Take the

---

remains unclear. In some manner the fire was not pleasing to the Lord. Perhaps they substituted embers from another source, thus cutting corners and violating the integrity of the altar fire. Other suggestions include acting at the wrong time, not being properly vested, or even being intoxicated while on duty (see v. 9). Whatever the case, the penalty of death reminds the people that God sees into the heart and makes strict demands of priestly service. Further, the poetic statement in verse 3 is telling. It juxtaposes holiness and glory as divine attributes. Holiness is the intrinsic characteristic of God; glory is God's extrinsic expression in creation: "Holy, holy, holy is the LORD of hosts! / All the earth is filled with his glory!" (Isa 6:3).

10:6-11 Conduct of the priests

Moses tells Aaron and his sons not to engage in mourning, leaving that duty to the people. Because contact with a corpse defiles a person, priests are to stay away except in the case of a next of kin (21:1-4; cf. Luke 10:31-32 [The Good Samaritan]). Notably, this is one time in Leviticus where Aaron speaks face to face with the Lord and not through Moses. The prohibition

grain offering left over from the oblations to the LORD, and eat it beside the altar in the form of unleavened cakes, since it is most holy. [13]You must eat it in a sacred place because it is your and your sons' due from the oblations to the LORD; such is the command I have received. [14]The brisket of the elevated offering and the leg of the contribution, however, you and your sons and daughters may eat, in a clean place; for these have been assigned to you and your children as your due from the communion sacrifices of the Israelites. [15]The leg of the contribution and the brisket of the elevated offering shall be brought in with the oblations of fat to be raised as an elevated offering before the LORD. They shall belong to you and your children as your due forever, as the LORD has commanded."

[16]Moses inquired closely about the goat of the purification offering and discovered that it had all been burned. So he was angry with the surviving sons of Aaron, Eleazar and Ithamar, and said, [17]"Why did you not eat the purification offering in the sacred place, since it is most holy? It has been given to you that

---

of alcohol probably relates to its impairing effects (Prov 20:1; 23:31-32; Hos 4:9-11). The most pointed condemnation of such abuse by those in leadership roles occurs in Isaiah: "Priest and prophet stagger from strong drink, / overpowered by wine; / They are confused by strong drink, / they stagger in their visions, / they totter when giving judgment" (28:7). This point flows into the following verses about the priest distinguishing the clean from the unclean and instructing the laws of the Lord to the Israelites. Impairment affects right judgment, so stay sober and alert.

In sum, this section speaks to a theology of priesthood. Privilege must not erode into being "intoxicated" by power and prestige. The priest is called from among the people, is accountable to the community, and is answerable before God. The priest is commissioned with *tôrâ* (instruction of the law), meaning that the people turn to him for understanding the Lord's will. This responsibility must be taken seriously because it impacts on the entire community; it does not remain insulated in a hidden sacred realm. Kingly duties are much the same. The king must exact justice impartially and is condemned for injustices (see 2 Sam 12:1-12 [Nathan judges King David]).

10:12-20 The eating of the priestly portions

This section focuses on the incident of the uneaten goat. Recalling the fate of Nadab and Abihu, the reader might expect divine wrath to fall upon these priests as well. However, Moses accepts the explanation of Aaron and his sons that fear of the Lord motivated their offering up the goat and not partaking of it (v. 19). Memory of the fate of Nadab and Abihu may account for the actions of these priests.

you might remove the guilt of the community and make atonement for them before the LORD. [18]Since its blood was not brought inside the sanctuary, you should certainly have eaten the offering in the sanctuary, as I was commanded." [19]Aaron answered Moses, "Even though they presented their purification offering and burnt offering before the LORD today, still this misfortune has befallen me. Had I then eaten of the purification offering today, would it have been pleasing to the LORD?" [20]On hearing this, Moses was satisfied.

III. Laws Regarding Ritual Purity

11 **Clean and Unclean Meats.** [1]The LORD said to Moses and Aaron:

Once again Moses acts as judge in a tense situation. One can justify Moses' anger at their insubordination because eating the priestly portion is required and not optional. The priest eating his portion serves to "swallow up" the unholy and is essential to the efficacy of the ritual. Although the precise interpretation of this section remains obscure, one may suggest that the integrity of the purification offering, entirely offered up to God, supersedes any questions about portions to the priest. Moses' satisfaction with Aaron's explanation is stated but not explained.

The incident juxtaposes clear laws and non-compliance to those laws, a tension that highlights the fragile and sometimes dangerous nature of human encounter with the divine. Further, this episode bespeaks divine and human freedom. God can have a change of heart, e.g., Adam and Eve never die for eating the forbidden fruit (Gen 2:17; 3:3-4). Humans can change their mind as Moses does here.

The tense and somewhat unhappy ending to chapter 10 seems awkward, but it certainly sets the stage for chapters 11–16 that deal with issues of purity. The priests must clearly understand their role and duties if they expect to judge rightly between the clean and unclean. Issues surrounding clear categories, proper boundaries, and distinct identities come into play with legal purity. The situations are different but the principles are much the same.

LAWS REGARDING RITUAL PURITY

Leviticus 11–16

This section discusses topics of which Leviticus is most popularly associated, i.e., ancient customs and matters of daily life. To the modern reader such detailed attention to unclean food, defilement at childbirth, leprosy, personal hygiene, and scapegoats seems primitive and superstitious. However, as with

²Speak to the Israelites and tell them: Of all land animals these are the ones you may eat: ³Any animal that has hoofs you may eat, provided it is cloven-footed and chews the cud. ⁴But you shall not eat any of the following from among those that only chew the cud or only have hoofs: the camel, which indeed chews the cud, but does not have hoofs and is therefore unclean for you; ⁵the rock hyrax, which indeed chews the cud, but does not have hoofs and is therefore unclean for you; ⁶the hare, which indeed chews the cud, but does not have hoofs and is therefore unclean for you; ⁷and the pig, which does indeed have hoofs and is cloven-footed, but does not chew the cud and is therefore unclean for you. ⁸You shall not eat their meat, and you shall not touch their carcasses; they are unclean for you.

⁹Of the various creatures that live in the water, you may eat the following: whatever in the seas or in river waters that has both fins and scales you may eat. ¹⁰But of the creatures that swarm in the water or of animals that otherwise live in the water, whether in the sea or in the rivers, all those that lack either fins

---

the ceremony of ordination, the *values* underlying these laws are timeless. The reader must remember that purity and holiness underlie these regulations.

The origins of clean and unclean things are rooted in a variety of needs and experiences, no one of which can be deemed definitive. Anthropologically, some foods become forbidden because they easily spoil and cause illness. Others do not fit into distinct categories and thus seem abnormal, such as reptiles that dwell both in water and on land, and birds that cannot fly. Animals that eat carrion consume what is dead and thus unclean. Boundaries are also involved. Skin lesions cross the boundaries of inner and outer parts of the body. Something is out of order. Theologically, order shows itself in fidelity to the categories and boundaries of creation (Gen 1, the Priestly account). God made birds of the air, fishes of the sea, and the land animals. Phenomena that blur this order are abnormal and unclean. They bespeak primordial chaos.

In sum, purity and holiness comprise more than personal and social hygiene. These values are at once physical, ritual, and moral, all demonstrating obedience to God. Holiness demands wholeness. This obedience harks back to the intentionality of creation in Genesis 1–2. Human dominion over other creatures includes a sense of limits and commitment to stewardship (Gen 1:28-31; 9:1-7).

11:1-23 Clean and unclean meats

This section echoes the classes of animals in Genesis 1: water, land, and flying creatures (cf. Deut 14:4-21). Edible land animals must be cloven-footed and chew the cud. These standards thus exclude the pig and the

or scales are loathsome for you, [11]and shall always be loathsome to you. Their meat you shall not eat, and their carcasses you shall loathe. [12]Every water creature that lacks fins or scales is loathsome for you.

[13]Of the birds, these you shall loathe; they shall not be eaten, they are loathsome: the griffon vulture, the bearded vulture, the black vulture, [14]the kite, the various species of falcons, [15]the various species of crows, [16]the eagle owl, the kestrel, the long-eared owl, the various species of hawks, [17]the little owl, the cormorant, the screech owl, [18]the barn owl, the horned owl, the osprey, [19]the stork, the various species of herons, the hoopoe, and the bat.

[20]The various winged insects that walk on all fours are loathsome for you.

---

camel. The ancient world did not have the sophisticated biology of fauna we have today, so some of the biblical understanding of animals is imprecise. For example, the hare reputedly chews the cud (v. 6). This error is based on the sideways chewing habits of the animal and not actual cud behavior. The bat is listed among the birds, though it is a mammal (v. 19). Clean water creatures have both fins and scales. Hence, scale-less water scavengers and shellfish are forbidden. The list of forbidden birds embodies three taboos. They are either flightless, predatory raptors, or eat carrion. Winged insects that hop on hind legs are edible (v. 22). All others that swarm or crawl on all fours are forbidden.

In sum, one must avoid the abnormal in creation. Land animals walk on all fours; fish swim with fins and have gills; and birds fly with wings and walk on hind legs. The primary concern is properly distinguishing what God deems clean or unclean in the created order (v. 47).

Not to be lost in the details of this chapter is the fact that God's covenant extends through all creation. It is significant that Genesis 1 depicts the created order as essentially vegetarian: "See, I give you every seed-bearing plant . . ." (1:29-30). Not until the great flood and covenant with Noah does violence among the creatures emerge: "Any living creature that moves about shall be yours to eat; I give them all to you as I did the green plants" (Gen 9:3).

This theological perspective helps the reader understand the laws enjoined here. The wanton and unregulated consumption of meat is forbidden from "the beginning" (Gen 1:1) and violates the call for humankind to be stewards of creation (Gen 1:26). The message of the prophets includes a dream of the initial harmony in creation: "Then the wolf shall be a guest of the lamb . . ." (Isa 11:6-9). That harmony would be characterized by peace and justice in the world. Indeed, a theology of ecology emerges from Leviticus 11.

39

²¹But of the various winged insects that walk on all fours you may eat those that have legs jointed above their feet for leaping on the ground; ²²hence of these you may eat the following: the various kinds of locusts, the various kinds of bald locusts, the various kinds of crickets, and the various kinds of grasshoppers. ²³All other winged insects that have four legs are loathsome for you.

²⁴You become unclean by the following—anyone who touches their carcasses shall be unclean until evening, ²⁵and anyone who carries any part of their carcasses shall wash his garments and be unclean until evening— ²⁶by all hoofed animals that are not cloven-footed or do not chew the cud; they are unclean for you; anyone who touches them becomes unclean. ²⁷Also by the various quadrupeds that walk on paws; they are unclean for you; anyone who touches their carcasses shall be unclean until evening, ²⁸and anyone who carries their carcasses shall wash his garments and be unclean until evening. They are unclean for you.

²⁹Of the creatures that swarm on the ground, the following are unclean for you: the rat, the mouse, the various kinds of lizards, ³⁰the gecko, the spotted lizard, the agama, the skink, and the chameleon. ³¹Among the various swarming creatures, these are unclean for you. Everyone who touches them when they are dead shall be unclean until evening. ³²Everything on which one of them falls when dead becomes unclean, including any article of wood, cloth, leather or goat hair—any article of which use can be made. It must be immersed in water and remain unclean until evening, when it again becomes clean. ³³Should any of these creatures fall into a clay vessel, everything in it becomes unclean, and the vessel itself you must break. ³⁴Any

11:24-47 Pollution by animals

This section moves from what may be consumed to what may be touched. The main point is the taboo of any dead creature, regardless of its cleanness in life. Those contaminated by the dead must bathe and remain unclean until the evening (v. 24). Contaminated earthenware vessels must be shattered (cf. 6:21). An exception is given to springs and cisterns (v. 36). These natural bodies provide water from the ground or from rain. Their connection with the waters of God's ordered creation makes them distinct and ever pure, unless contaminated by humans.

The repeated rationale for all these laws is the divine holiness in which only the pure may share. Everything holy remains "apart" in some way: apart from the pagan nations, apart from uncleanness as God commands, and set apart in communal morality and personal vocation. The words in 10:10 state it all succinctly: "You must be able to distinguish between what is sacred and what is profane, and between what is clean and what is unclean."

food that can be eaten which makes contact with water, and any liquid that may be drunk, in any such vessel become unclean. 35Any object on which any part of their carcasses falls becomes unclean; if it is an oven or stove, this must be broken to pieces; they are unclean and shall always be unclean to you. 36However, a spring or a cistern for collecting water remains clean; but whoever touches such an animal's carcass becomes unclean. 37If any part of their carcasses falls on any sort of grain that is to be sown, it remains clean; 38but if the grain has become moistened, it becomes unclean to you when any part of their carcasses falls on it.

39When one of the animals that you could otherwise eat dies of itself, anyone who touches its carcass shall be unclean until evening; 40and anyone who eats any part of its carcass shall wash his garments and be unclean until evening; so also, anyone who carries its carcass shall wash his garments and be unclean until evening.

41All the creatures that swarm on the ground are loathsome and shall not be eaten. 42Whether it crawls on its belly, goes on all fours, or has many legs—any creature that swarms on the earth—you shall not eat them; they are loathsome. 43Do not make yourselves loathsome by any swarming creature nor defile yourselves with them and so become unclean by them. 44For I, the LORD, am your God. You shall make and keep yourselves holy, because I am holy. You shall not make yourselves unclean, then, by any swarming creature that crawls on the ground. 45Since I, the LORD, am the one who brought you up from the land of Egypt that I might be your God, you shall be holy, because I am holy.

46This is the instruction for land animals, birds, and all the creatures that move about in the water, as well as any animal that swarms on the ground, 47that you may distinguish between the clean and the unclean, and between creatures that may be eaten and those that may not be eaten.

12 **Uncleanness of Childbirth.** 1The LORD said to Moses: 2Tell the Israelites: When a woman has a child, giving birth to a boy, she shall be unclean for seven days, with the same uncleanness as during her menstrual period. 3On the eighth day, the flesh of the boy's foreskin shall be circumcised, 4and then she shall spend thirty-three days more in a state of blood purity; she shall not touch anything sacred nor enter the sanctuary till the days of her purification are fulfilled. 5If she gives birth to a girl, for fourteen days she shall be as unclean as

12:1-8 Uncleanness of childbirth

Behind the laws enjoined here is the value of life from cradle to grave. Life is in the blood (17:11; Deut 12:23), a belief that pervades the Scriptures. To understand this law the modern reader should call to mind the common human reaction to the sight of blood. Bleeding is typically abnormal and a sign of something dangerous at work in the body or violence done to it from the outside. The ancients shared such emotional reaction and gave blood

during her menstrual period, after which she shall spend sixty-six days in a state of blood purity.

⁶When the days of her purification for a son or for a daughter are fulfilled, she shall bring to the priest at the entrance of the tent of meeting a yearling lamb for a burnt offering and a pigeon or a turtledove for a purification offering. ⁷The priest shall offer them before the LORD to make atonement for her, and thus she will be clean again after her flow of blood. Such is the ritual for the woman who gives birth to a child, male or female. ⁸If, however, she cannot afford a lamb, she may take two turtledoves or two pigeons, the one for a burnt offering and the other for a purification offering. The priest shall make atonement for her, and thus she will again be clean.

13 Scaly Infection. ¹The LORD said to Moses and Aaron: ²When someone has on the skin a mark, lesion, or blotch which appears to develop into a scaly infection, the person shall be brought to Aaron, the priest, or to one of the priests among his sons. ³If the priest, upon examination of the skin's infection, finds that the hair on the infection has turned white and the infection itself appears to be deeper than the skin, it is indeed a scaly infection; the priest, on seeing this, shall declare the person unclean. ⁴If, however, the blotch on the skin is white, but does not seem to be deeper than the skin, nor has the hair turned white, the priest shall quarantine the af-

---

a rich variety of meanings. It was at once the source of life and a symbol of death. It is bright red and stains what it touches. It also has the ability to ward off evil (see Exod 12:21-23 [Passover blood]). Hence, one must not dismiss as superstitious what are innate and pervasive ideas in the human psyche. Some people even faint at the sight of blood.

The blood of menstruation and childbirth ultimately bespeaks holiness, not displeasure or rejection. The emphasis is not on defilement but purification and restoration. Blood "defilement" here is a condition that must be set aright to bring healing and harmony to the family and community. During childbirth blood unites life and death in a mysterious tension. Miscarriage and infant mortality were high in the ancient world, so the survival of mother or child was fragile, fraught with mystery and bittersweet experience. These realities and emotions inform the meaning of this passage. The events that follow childbirth (circumcision of a son and the purification of the mother) guarantee purity, social harmony, and the hope of a happy life for all involved. May all enjoy peace (*shālôm*).

13:1-59 Scaly infection

This lengthy chapter addresses a variety of skin diseases, none of which can be associated directly with leprosy (Hansen's disease). Skin ailments

flicted person for seven days. ⁵Should the priest, upon examination on the seventh day, find that the infection has remained unchanged in color and has not spread on the skin, the priest shall quarantine the person for another seven days. ⁶Should the priest, upon examination again on the seventh day, find that the infection is now faded and has not spread on the skin, the priest shall declare the person clean; it was merely a scab. The person shall wash his garments and so become clean. ⁷But if, after the person was examined by the priest and declared clean, the scab spreads at all on the skin, the person shall once more be examined by the priest. ⁸Should the priest, upon examination, find that the scab has indeed spread on the skin, he shall declare the person unclean; it is a scaly infection.

⁹When someone is afflicted with a scaly infection, that person shall be brought to the priest. ¹⁰Should the priest, upon examination, find that there is a white mark on the skin which has turned the hair white and that there is raw flesh in it, ¹¹it is a chronic scaly infection on the skin. The priest shall declare the person unclean without quarantine, since the individual is certainly unclean. ¹²If the scaly infection breaks out on the skin and, as far as the priest can see, covers all the skin of the afflicted person from head to foot, ¹³should the priest then, upon examination, find that the scaly infection does cover the whole body, he shall declare the afflicted person clean; since the person has turned completely white; that individual is clean. ¹⁴But as soon as raw flesh appears, the individual is unclean; ¹⁵on observing the raw flesh, the priest shall declare the person unclean, because raw flesh is unclean; it is a scaly infection. ¹⁶If, however, the raw flesh again turns white, the person shall return to the priest; ¹⁷should the latter, upon examination, find that the infection has indeed turned white, he shall declare the afflicted person clean; the individual is clean.

¹⁸If a boil appeared on a person's skin which later healed, ¹⁹should now in the place of the boil a white mark or a reddish white blotch develop, the person shall be examined by the priest. ²⁰If the latter, upon examination, finds that it is deeper than the skin and that the hair has turned white, he shall declare the person unclean; it is a scaly infection that has broken out in the boil. ²¹But if the priest, upon examination, finds that there is no white hair in it and that it is not deeper than the skin and is faded, the priest shall quarantine the person for seven days. ²²If it has then spread on the skin, the priest shall declare the person unclean; it is an infection. ²³But if the blotch remains the same without spreading, it is merely the scar of the boil; the priest shall therefore declare the person clean.

---

render persons unclean, with consequences that ostracize them from the community for shorter or longer periods (vv. 4 and 45-46). The chapter is divided into several sets of criteria: diseases of the skin, scars, burns, hair problems, and even articles of clothing. Houses can be "leprous" as well (14:33-57).

²⁴If there was a burn on a person's skin, and the burned area now becomes a reddish white or a white blotch, ²⁵when the priest, upon examination, finds that the hair has turned white in the blotch and this seems to be deeper than the skin, it is a scaly infection that has broken out in the burn; the priest shall therefore declare the person unclean; it is a scaly infection. ²⁶But if the priest, upon examination, finds that there is no white hair in the blotch and that this is not deeper than the skin and is faded, the priest shall quarantine the person for seven days. ²⁷Should the priest, upon examination on the seventh day, find that it has spread at all on the skin, he shall declare the person unclean; it is a scaly infection. ²⁸But if the blotch remains the same without spreading on the skin and is faded, it is merely the spot of the burn; the priest shall therefore declare the person clean, since it is only the scar of the burn.

²⁹When a man or a woman has an infection on the head or in the beard, ³⁰should the priest, upon examination, find that the infection appears to be deeper than the skin and that there is fine yellow hair in it, the priest shall declare the person unclean; it is a scall. It is a scaly infection of the head or beard. ³¹But if the priest, upon examining the scall infection, finds that it does not appear to be deeper than the skin, though the hair in it may not be black, the priest shall quarantine the scall-stricken person for seven days. ³²Should the priest, upon examining the infection on the seventh day find that the scall has not spread and has no yellow hair in it and does not seem to be deeper than the skin, ³³the person shall shave, but not the scall spot. Then the priest shall quarantine the scall-diseased person for another seven days. ³⁴If the priest, upon examining the scall on the seventh day, finds that it has not spread on the skin and that it does not appear to be deeper than the skin, he shall declare the person clean; the latter shall wash his garments, and will thus be clean. ³⁵But if the scall spreads at all on the skin after the person has been declared clean—³⁶should the priest, upon examination, find that the scall has indeed spread on the skin, he need not look for yellow hair; the individual is unclean. ³⁷If, however, the scall has remained unchanged in color and black hair has grown in it, the disease has been healed; the person is clean, and the priest shall declare the individual clean.

³⁸When the skin of a man or a woman is spotted with several white blotches, ³⁹if the priest, upon examination, finds that the blotches on the skin are pale

---

It is noteworthy that the accusation of sin is absent in this chapter. Although skin disease may be the result of sin, it is not necessarily so. One can surmise that eruptions of the skin were so common in the ancient world that one could hardly presume a connection with sin. On the one hand, no one wanted to contract the disease by proximity or touching. On the other hand, drawing the afflicted person back into the community was a value. Probably victims of skin disease were more pitied than judged.

white, it is only tetter that has broken out on the skin, and the person therefore is clean.

⁴⁰When a man loses the hair of his head, he is simply bald on the crown and not unclean. ⁴¹So too, if he loses the hair on the front of his head, he is simply bald on the forehead and not unclean. ⁴²But when there is a reddish white infection on his bald crown or bald forehead, it is a scaly infection that is breaking out there. ⁴³If the priest, upon examination, finds that the infection spot on the bald area on the crown or forehead has the same reddish white appearance as that of a scaly infection of the skin, ⁴⁴the man has a scaly infection and is unclean. The priest shall declare him unclean; his infection is on his head.

⁴⁵The garments of one afflicted with a scaly infection shall be rent and the hair disheveled, and the mustache covered. The individual shall cry out, "Unclean, unclean!" ⁴⁶As long as the infection is present, the person shall be unclean. Being unclean, that individual shall dwell apart, taking up residence outside the camp.

Fungal Infection of Fabrics and Leather. ⁴⁷When a fungal infection is on a garment of wool or of linen, ⁴⁸or on the warp and woof of linen or wool, or on a hide or anything made of leather, ⁴⁹if the infection on the garment or hide, or on the warp or woof, or on any leather ar-ticle is greenish or reddish, the thing is indeed a fungal infection and must be examined by the priest. ⁵⁰Having examined the infection, the priest shall quarantine the infected article for seven days. ⁵¹If the priest, upon inspecting the infection on the seventh day, finds that it has spread on the garment, or on the warp or woof, or on the leather, whatever be its use, the infection is a harmful fungus; the article is unclean. ⁵²He shall therefore burn up the garment, or the warp or woof, be it of wool or linen, or any leather article which is infected; since it is a harmful fungus, it must be destroyed by fire. ⁵³But if the priest, upon examination, finds that it has not spread on the garment, or on the warp or woof, or on the leather article, ⁵⁴he shall give orders to have the infected article washed and then quarantined for another seven days. ⁵⁵If the priest, upon examination after the infection was washed, finds that it has not changed its color, even though it may not have spread, the article is unclean. You shall burn it with fire. It is a fray, be it on its inner or outer side. ⁵⁶But if the priest, upon examination, finds that the infection has faded after the washing, he shall cut it out of the garment, or the leather, or the warp or woof. ⁵⁷If, however, the infection again appears on the garment, or on the warp or woof, or on the leather article, it is still virulent and you shall burn the thing

---

The tragedy of such conditions shows itself in other biblical passages. So-called lepers wander in bands (2 Kgs 7:1-13) and are shunned no matter their status in life (2 Kgs 5:1-27; 2 Chr 26:16-21). In the New Testament Jesus shows compassion to lepers and enjoins his disciples to care for them (Mark 1:41; Matt 10:8).

infected with fire. [58]But if, after the washing, the infection has disappeared from the garment, or the warp or woof, or the leather article, the thing shall be washed a second time, and thus it will be clean. [59]This is the instruction for a fungal infection on a garment of wool or linen, or on a warp or woof, or on any leather article, to determine whether it is clean or unclean.

14 **Purification After Scaly Infection.** [1]The LORD said to Moses: [2]This is the ritual for someone that had a scaly infection at the time of that person's purification. The individual shall be brought to the priest, [3]who is to go outside the camp. If the priest, upon inspection, finds that the scaly infection has healed in the afflicted person, [4]he shall order that two live, clean birds, as well as some cedar wood, scarlet yarn, and hyssop be obtained for the one who is to be purified. [5]The priest shall then order that one of the birds be slaughtered over an earthen vessel with fresh water in it. [6]Taking the living bird with the cedar wood, the scarlet yarn and the hyssop, the priest shall dip them, including the live bird, in the blood of the bird that was slaughtered over the fresh water, [7]and then sprinkle seven times on the person to be purified from the scaly infection. When he has thus purified that person, he shall let the living bird fly away over the countryside. [8]The person being purified shall then wash his garments, shave off all hair, and bathe in water, and so become clean. After this the person may come inside the camp, but shall still remain outside his or her tent for seven days. [9]On the seventh day this individual shall again shave off all hair, of the head, beard, and eyebrows— all hair must be shaved—and also wash his garments and bathe the body in water, and so become clean.

[10]On the eighth day the individual shall take two unblemished male lambs, one unblemished yearling ewe lamb, three tenths of an ephah of bran flour

---

In sum, the pervasiveness of skin disease in life and its variety of manifestations commends such diseases to the interests of Leviticus. To be holy means to be whole and without *dis*-ease. What modern society would refer to physicians, they referred to priests. Their perspective is surely primitive, but every age grapples with diseases it does not understand and that can evoke panic among the people and ostracism of the victims. One thinks of HIV, SARS, avian bird flu, and other diseases today. Social lepers in every age are often the victims of misinformation and false labeling.

14:1-57 Purification after scaly infection

This section builds on chapter 13 and addresses how to deal with cured scaly infections and the victim's ritual purification. It is important to note that culpability is not a central issue. Rather, those ostracized are drawn back inside the camp from which they were excluded. Such persons are no longer "outside the camp" (v. 3).

mixed with oil for a grain offering, and one log of oil. ¹¹The priest who performs the purification ceremony shall place the person who is being purified, as well as all these offerings, before the Lord at the entrance of the tent of meeting. ¹²Taking one of the male lambs, the priest shall present it as a reparation offering, along with the log of oil, raising them as an elevated offering before the Lord. ¹³This lamb shall be slaughtered in the sacred place where the purification offering and the burnt offering are slaughtered, because the reparation offering is like the purification offering; it belongs to the priest and is most holy. ¹⁴Then the priest shall take some of the blood of the reparation offering and put it on the lobe of the right ear, the thumb of the right hand, and the big toe of the right foot of the person being purified. ¹⁵The priest shall also take the log of oil and pour some of it into the palm of his own left hand; ¹⁶then, dipping his right finger in the oil on his left palm, he shall sprinkle some of it with his finger seven times before the Lord. ¹⁷Of the oil left in his hand the priest shall put some on the lobe of the right ear, the thumb of the right hand, and the big toe of the right foot of the person being purified, over the blood of the reparation offering. ¹⁸The rest of the oil in his hand the priest shall put on the head of the one being purified. Thus shall the priest make atonement for the individual before the Lord. ¹⁹The priest shall next offer the purification offering, thus making atonement on behalf of the one being purified from the uncleanness. After this the burnt offering shall be slaughtered. ²⁰The priest shall offer the burnt offering and the grain offering on the altar before the Lord. Thus shall the priest make atonement for the person, and the individual will become clean.

Poor Person's Sacrifices. ²¹If a person is poor and cannot afford so much, that person shall take one male lamb for a reparation offering, to be used as an elevated offering in atonement, one tenth of an ephah of bran flour mixed with oil for a grain offering, a log of oil, ²²and two turtledoves or pigeons, which the individual can more easily afford, the one as a purification offering and the other as a burnt offering. ²³On the eighth day of purification the person shall bring them to the priest, at the entrance of the tent of meeting before the Lord. ²⁴Taking the

---

The length of the purification ritual and its stages are noteworthy. The process begins outside the camp and moves toward the camp. The list of items for the ritual is specific: two birds, cedar wood, scarlet yarn, and hyssop. One bird is sacrificed; the other is set free as a sign of the person's restoration (cf. 16:20-28, the scapegoat). The malady is symbolically carried off. The wood, yarn, and hyssop are used to fashion a sprinkler to splash the blood mixed with spring water. The sevenfold sprinkling bespeaks perfection and wholeness. The person is now restored to the community. In sum, purification and atonement are the heart of the ritual as reiterated in verses 8, 9, and 20.

lamb of the reparation offering, along with the log of oil, the priest shall raise them as an elevated offering before the LORD. ²⁵When the lamb of the reparation offering has been slaughtered, the priest shall take some of its blood, and put it on the lobe of the right ear, on the thumb of the right hand, and on the big toe of the right foot of the person being purified. ²⁶The priest shall then pour some of the oil into the palm of his own left hand ²⁷and with his right finger sprinkle some of the oil in his left palm seven times before the LORD. ²⁸Some of the oil in his hand the priest shall also put on the lobe of the right ear, the thumb of the right hand, and the big toe of the right foot of the person being purified, where he had sprinkled the blood of the reparation offering. ²⁹The rest of the oil in his hand the priest shall put on the head of the one being purified. Thus shall he make atonement for the individual before the LORD. ³⁰Then, of the turtledoves or pigeons, such as the person can afford, ³¹the priest shall offer one as a purifica-

tion offering and the other as a burnt offering, along with the grain offering. Thus shall the priest make atonement before the LORD for the person who is being purified. ³²This is the ritual for one afflicted with a scaly infection who has insufficient means for purification.

Fungal Infection of Houses. ³³The LORD said to Moses and Aaron: ³⁴When you come into the land of Canaan, which I am giving you to possess, if I put a fungal infection in any house of the land you occupy, ³⁵the owner of the house shall come and report to the priest, "Something like an infection has appeared in my house." ³⁶The priest shall then order the house to be cleared out before he goes in to examine the infection, lest everything in the house become unclean. Only after this is he to go in to examine the house. ³⁷If the priest, upon inspection, finds that the infection on the walls of the house consists of greenish or reddish spots which seem to go deeper than the surface of the wall, ³⁸he shall go out of the house to the doorway

Purification follows with a sacrifice on the eighth day. Animals, grain, and oil are involved. Since sensitivity to the poor is a value in Leviticus, doves or pigeons may be substituted for lambs (vv. 21-32). The sacrifice is one of thanksgiving but also one of precaution. The affliction may have been coincidental or may have been occasioned by some offense unknown to the victim. Cover all the bases.

By extension scaly infection can infect dwellings and their contents (vv. 33-57). Probably mold, mildew, and rust are involved. The fact that these conditions are often bright in color, spread across surfaces, and are hard to scrub off lends to the perception that they are "leprous" like skin infections. Pagan cultures attributed such nuisances to demonic powers. Ancient Israel believed that God created all things and can use all things to teach and punish (v. 34).

and quarantine the house for seven days. ³⁹On the seventh day the priest shall return. If, upon inspection, he finds that the infection has spread on the walls, ⁴⁰he shall order the infected stones to be pulled out and cast in an unclean place outside the city. ⁴¹The whole inside of the house shall then be scraped, and the mortar that has been scraped off shall be dumped in an unclean place outside the city. ⁴²Then other stones shall be brought and put in the place of the old stones, and new mortar obtained and plastered on the house. ⁴³If the infection breaks out once more in the house after the stones have been pulled out and the house has been scraped and replastered, ⁴⁴the priest shall come; and if, upon inspection, he finds that the infection has spread in the house, it is a corrosive fungus in the house, and it is unclean. ⁴⁵It shall be pulled down, and all its stones, beams and mortar shall be hauled away to an unclean place outside the city. ⁴⁶Whoever enters a house while it is quarantined shall be unclean until evening. ⁴⁷Whoever sleeps or eats in such a house shall also wash his garments.

⁴⁸If the priest finds, when he comes to the house, that the infection has in fact not spread in the house after the plastering, he shall declare the house clean, since the infection has been healed. ⁴⁹To purify the house, he shall take two birds, as well as cedar wood, scarlet yarn, and hyssop. ⁵⁰One of the birds he shall slaughter over an earthen vessel with fresh water in it. ⁵¹Then, taking the cedar wood, the hyssop and the scarlet yarn, together with the living bird, he shall dip them all in the blood of the slaughtered bird and the fresh water, and sprinkle the house seven times. ⁵²Thus he shall purify the house with the bird's blood and the fresh water, along with the living bird, the cedar wood, the hyssop, and the scarlet yarn. ⁵³He shall then let the living bird fly away over the countryside outside the city. Thus he shall make atonement for the house, and it will be clean.

⁵⁴This is the ritual for every kind of human scaly infection and scall, ⁵⁵and for fungus diseases in garments and houses—⁵⁶for marks, lesions and blotches—⁵⁷to give direction when there

---

Further, the house or home (Hebrew *bēth*) in biblical theology is more than a structure. It bespeaks the family and its members. The home is the dwelling where sabbaths and annual Passovers are observed. Home is the locus of hospitality. Care for the purity of the house symbolized the integrity of the family. It is noteworthy that synagogues are often named as "House of . . .," e.g., Beth El (House of God), Beth Shalom (House of Peace), and Beth Israel (House of Israel).

The summary in verses 54-57 wraps up the scaly infection laws in chapters 13–14. The importance of cleanness is reiterated as a criterion of holiness. Skin disease and mold on surfaces bespeak disorder and "*dis*-ease," i.e., loss of health, stress, and even intimations of death. The priest must be familiar with these phenomena and diagnose them rightly.

is a state of uncleanness and when a state of cleanness. This is the ritual for scaly infection.

15 **Sexual Uncleanness.** ¹The LORD said to Moses and Aaron: ²Speak to the Israelites and tell them: When any man has a genital discharge, he is thereby unclean. ³Such is his uncleanness from this discharge, whether his body drains freely with the discharge or is blocked up from the discharge. His uncleanness is on him all the days that his body discharges or is blocked up from his discharge; this is his uncleanness. ⁴Any bed on which the man with the discharge lies is unclean, and any article on which he sits is unclean. ⁵Anyone who touches his bed shall wash his garments, bathe in water, and be unclean until evening. ⁶Whoever sits on an article on which the man with the discharge was sitting shall wash his garments, bathe in water, and be unclean until evening. ⁷Whoever touches the body of the man with the discharge shall wash his garments, bathe in water, and be unclean until evening. ⁸If the man with the discharge spits on a clean person, the latter shall wash his garments, bathe in water, and be unclean until evening. ⁹Any saddle on which the man with the discharge rides is unclean. ¹⁰Whoever touches anything that was under him shall be unclean until evening; whoever carries any such thing shall wash his garments, bathe in water, and be unclean until evening. ¹¹Anyone whom the man with the discharge touches with his unrinsed hands shall wash his garments, bathe in water, and be unclean until evening. ¹²Earthenware touched by the man with the discharge shall be broken; and every wooden article shall be rinsed with water.

15:1-33 Sexual uncleanness

These laws resume the topic of childbirth (ch. 12) but relate more directly to male and female emissions and matters of intercourse. The process of purification for men and of women parallel one another in the narrative (cf. vv. 1-18, 19-30).

The modern reader must not assume a universal and timeless understanding of sexual morality. Sexuality in every culture enjoys a unique understanding and canons of appropriate and inappropriate behavior. Again, the priestly tradition that underlies much of Leviticus is informed by Genesis 1 and the divinely blessed human stewardship of all creation stated therein (Gen 1:26-28). Sexual union that brings life is godly by its very nature; no view of sexuality as dirty or a tolerated sin for the sake of procreation can be found here. Ancient reproductive science was primitive by our standards. The male fertilized the woman, and she as the "nest" produced the child. Hence, one never reads of barren men in the Bible, only barren women. Yet an appreciation of the mystery and the holiness of life remains a timeless value.

¹³When a man with a discharge becomes clean of his discharge, he shall count seven days for his purification. Then he shall wash his garments and bathe his body in fresh water, and so he will be clean. ¹⁴On the eighth day he shall take two turtledoves or two pigeons, and going before the Lord, to the entrance of the tent of meeting, he shall give them to the priest, ¹⁵who shall offer them up, the one as a purification offering and the other as a burnt offering. Thus shall the priest make atonement before the Lord for the man because of his discharge.

¹⁶When a man has an emission of semen, he shall bathe his whole body in water and be unclean until evening. ¹⁷Any piece of cloth or leather with semen on it shall be washed with water and be unclean until evening.

¹⁸If a man has sexual relations with a woman, they shall both bathe in water and be unclean until evening.

¹⁹When a woman has a flow of blood from her body, she shall be in a state of menstrual uncleanness for seven days. Anyone who touches her shall be unclean until evening. ²⁰Anything on which she lies or sits during her menstrual period shall be unclean. ²¹Anyone who touches her bed shall wash his garments, bathe in water, and be unclean until evening. ²²Whoever touches any article on which she was sitting shall wash his garments, bathe in water, and be unclean until evening. ²³Whether an object is on the bed or on something she sat upon, when the person touches it, that person shall be unclean until evening. ²⁴If a man lies with her, he contracts her menstrual uncleanness and shall be unclean for seven days; every bed on which he then lies also becomes unclean.

²⁵When a woman has a flow of blood for several days outside her menstrual period, or when her flow continues

Chapter 15 teaches that the mysteries of physical sexuality expressed in genders, male and female, are gifts that bind God and humankind together. An essential aspect of blessing is fertility: "God blessed them and God said to them: Be fertile and multiply; fill the earth and subdue it" (Gen 1:28). Blessing shines forth in children, abundant flocks and fields, a good name in the community, and ultimately peace: "May the Lord bless you from Zion, / may you see Jerusalem's prosperity / all the days of your life, / and live to see your children's children. / Peace upon Israel!" (Ps 128:5-6).

Personal uncleanness of men comes from an ongoing genital discharge, probably referring to symptoms of gonorrhea and related sexually transmitted diseases. The striking distinction of this impurity is that the victim can remain in the community and at home, not banished outside the camp as with leprosy. Genital area contact with objects such as a bed, chair, or saddle makes those items unclean. Human to human physical contact and spitting also bring uncleanness. In sum, direct contact (or perceived direct contact) of the genital discharge with another person or object generates impurity.

beyond the ordinary period, as long as she suffers this unclean flow she shall be unclean, just as during her menstrual period. ²⁶Any bed on which she lies during such a flow becomes unclean, as it would during her menstrual period, and any article on which she sits becomes unclean just as during her menstrual period. ²⁷Anyone who touches them becomes unclean; that person shall wash his garments, bathe in water, and be unclean until evening.

²⁸When she becomes clean from her flow, she shall count seven days; after this she becomes clean. ²⁹On the eighth day she shall take two turtledoves or two pigeons and bring them to the priest at the entrance of the tent of meeting. ³⁰The priest shall offer one of them as a purification offering and the other as a burnt offering. Thus shall the priest make atonement before the LORD for her because of her unclean flow.

The meaning of verse 18 deserves comment because, if read superficially, it may appear to suggest that sexual union is immoral. The emissions associated with sexual intercourse, not the act itself, are the major issue as the surrounding material affirms. When a man gives his life-giving seed to the woman, there is no certainty that an offspring will be born. The potency of seminal discharge and the fragility of conception and birth create a delicate balance of life and death. In Leviticus it is appropriate that the partners bathe in water as an act of purification. Water is essential for life, cleanses what it touches, and offers refreshment and replenishment of energy. These associations underlie this law.

The counterpart to male seminal emission is the woman's menstruation. Both men and women are impure for seven days, and curiously the woman transmits her impurity to the man (vv. 13, 24). The reason for these designations is unclear. It may relate to the ambiguity of blood as both a symbol and instrument of life *and* death. Also the loss of powerful and life-giving fluids (semen and blood) may be in mind. The cure of uncontrolled menstruation is one of Jesus' miracles in the New Testament (Matt 9:20-22; Mark 5:25-34; Luke 8:43-48) and creates a foil to this law in Leviticus. Jesus is not made impure by the woman's contact but rather he purifies her. Jesus demonstrates the power to work a wonder that transcends the sacred law.

Verses 31-33 conclude this section. Emphasis is given to the fact that these laws prevent the defilement of sacred spaces, particularly the Lord's dwelling, also called the tabernacle or holy of holies. This summary leads nicely into the next section about the Day of Atonement. This festival was the grand occasion on which the high priest would sprinkle blood of the bull and goat on the mercy seat in the holy of holies.

[31]You shall warn the Israelites of their uncleanness, lest they die through their uncleanness by defiling my tabernacle, which is in their midst.

[32]This is the ritual for the man with a discharge, or who has an emission of semen, and thereby becomes unclean; [33]as well as for the woman who has her menstrual period; or one who has a discharge, male or female; and also for the man who lies with an unclean woman.

16 The Day of Atonement. [1]After the death of Aaron's two sons, who died when they encroached on the LORD's presence, the LORD spoke to Moses [2]and said to him: Tell your brother Aaron that he is not to come whenever he pleases into the inner sanctuary, inside the veil, in front of the cover on the ark, lest he die, for I reveal myself in a cloud above the ark's cover. [3]Only in this way may Aaron enter the inner sanctuary. He shall bring a bull of the herd for a purification offering and a ram for a burnt offering. [4]He shall wear the sacred linen tunic, with the linen pants underneath, gird himself with the linen sash and put on the linen turban. But since these vestments are sacred, he shall not put them on until he has first bathed his body in water. [5]From the Israelite community he shall receive two male goats for a purification offering and one ram for a burnt offering.

[6]Aaron shall offer the bull, his purification offering, to make atonement for himself and for his household. [7]Taking the two male goats and setting them before the LORD at the entrance of the tent of meeting, [8]he shall cast lots to determine which one is for the LORD and which for Azazel. [9]The goat that is determined by lot for the LORD, Aaron shall present and offer up as a purification offering. [10]But the goat determined by lot for Azazel he shall place before the LORD alive, so that with it he may make atonement by sending it off to Azazel in the desert.

[11]Thus shall Aaron offer his bull for the purification offering, to make atonement for himself and for his family. When he has slaughtered it, [12]he shall take a censer full of glowing embers from the altar before the LORD, as well as a double handful of finely ground fragrant incense, and bringing them

---

16:1-19 The Day of Atonement

The modern reader often associates Judaism with its annual observances, including the New Year (*rōsh hashānâ*) and the climactic Day of Atonement (*yôm kippûr*). This chapter speaks to these sacred calendared events of the fall harvest so deeply rooted in Israel's history and self-understanding. Some ideas borrowed from ancient Israel's surrounding neighbors may be behind these observances, e.g., the need to quell blood vengeance among clans and the exorcism of demons from a temple. However, the content and meaning of these observances sets Judaism apart and highlights the complexities of cultural borrowings and religious self-identification in any age.

inside the veil, [13]there before the LORD he shall put incense on the fire, so that a cloud of incense may shield the cover that is over the covenant, else he will die. [14]Taking some of the bull's blood, he shall sprinkle it with his finger on the front of the ark's cover and likewise sprinkle some of the blood with his finger seven times in front of the cover.

[15]Then he shall slaughter the goat of the people's purification offering, and bringing its blood inside the veil, he shall do with it as he did with the bull's blood, sprinkling it on the ark's cover and in front of it. [16]Thus he shall purge the inner sanctuary of all the Israelites' impurities and trespasses, including all their sins. He shall do the same for the tent of meeting, which is set up among them in the midst of their uncleanness. [17]No one else may be in the tent of meeting from the time he enters the inner sanctuary to make atonement until he departs. When he has made atonement for himself and his household, as well as for the whole Israelite assembly, [18]he shall come out to the altar before the LORD and purge it also. Taking some of the bull's and the goat's blood, he shall put it on the horns around the altar, [19]and with his finger sprinkle some of the blood on it seven times. Thus he

---

A day of atonement for priests and the people recognizes that the rituals cited in Leviticus have their effect, but the community must not overlook other acts of ritual impurity and personal sins that accumulate during the year. These, too, require purification or atonement. Further, the altar used for the offering of animals and cereals merits re-consecration over time.

Only on the Day of Atonement may the priest enter the inner sanctuary (Holy of Holies) to purify the sacred space. He cannot enter whenever he pleases (v. 2), a warning that harks back to the fate of Nadab and Abihu (10:1-2). Further, the priest must properly dress for the occasion and offer a bull for purification and atonement, followed by a sacrificial goat. The censer smoke and the sprinkling of blood on the ark and the people add to the solemnity.

The purification of the sanctuary begins in verse 11. Sprinkling of the animal blood is essential to the ritual. The priest brings the bull (v. 6); the people bring the goat (v. 15). The collective blood atones for the whole community, priests and laity alike. The abundant incense fills the holy of holies (vv. 12-13). The volume of smoke befits the utter holiness of the inner sanctum. It may also serve to shield the priest from gazing clearly about this sacred space lest he be struck dead (v. 13). The sprinkling of the animal bloods in the holy of holies is described in some detail (vv. 14-15). From there the priest moves to the altar and performs much the same ritual (vv. 18-19). He then purifies the people, the point where the scapegoat comes into play.

shall purify it and sanctify it from the impurities of the Israelites.

The Scapegoat. [20]When he has finished purging the inner sanctuary, the tent of meeting and the altar, Aaron shall bring forward the live goat. [21]Laying both hands on its head, he shall confess over it all the iniquities of the Israelites and their trespasses, including all their sins, and so put them on the goat's head. He shall then have it led into the wilderness by an attendant. [22]The goat will carry off all their iniquities to an isolated region.

When the goat is dispatched into the wilderness, [23]Aaron shall go into the tent of meeting, strip off the linen vestments he had put on when he entered the inner sanctuary, and leave them in the tent of meeting. [24]After bathing his body with water in a sacred place, he shall put on his regular vestments, and then come out and offer his own and the people's burnt offering, in atonement for himself and for the people, [25]and also burn the fat of the purification offering on the altar.

[26]The man who led away the goat for Azazel shall wash his garments and bathe his body in water; only then may he enter the camp. [27]The bull and the goat of the purification offering whose blood was brought to make atonement in the inner sanctuary, shall be taken outside the camp, where their hides and flesh and dung shall be burned in the fire. [28]The one who burns them shall wash his garments and bathe his body in water; only then may he enter the camp.

The Fast. [29]This shall be an everlasting statute for you: on the tenth day of the seventh month every one of you, whether a native or a resident alien, shall humble yourselves and shall do no work. [30]For on this day atonement is made for you to make you clean; of all your sins you will be cleansed before the LORD. [31]It shall be a sabbath of complete rest for you, on which you must humble yourselves—an everlasting statute.

16:20-28 The scapegoat

The scapegoat (Hebrew "goat for ʿăzāʾzēl," vv. 8, 10 [twice], 26) deserves some comment. A number of explanations of its meaning have been proposed. The animal may symbolically carry away the guilt of the people, or may represent a geographical location or formation. Probably Azazel is rooted in a legendary male demon of the desert evidenced in Mesopotamian literature. In the Scriptures this figure is merely symbolic and represents the removal of sin for all the people. The goat for Azazel is distinct from the sacrificial goat and selected by casting lots (v. 8). Casting lots leaves the choice of each goat's fate to the Lord's will. The laying on of both hands by the priest and sending of the goat into the wilderness "carries off" the burden of sins and restores spiritual and communal harmony. The desert has several meanings in the Scriptures, one of which is its being the place of sinners and evil spirits. This meaning applies here (cf. Isa 34:13-14; Matt 12:43).

³²This atonement is to be made by the priest who has been anointed and ordained to the priesthood in succession to his father. He shall wear the linen garments, the sacred vestments, ³³and purge the most sacred part of the sanctuary, as well as the tent of meeting, and the altar. He shall also make atonement for the priests and all the people of the assembly. ³⁴This, then, shall be an everlasting statute for you: once a year atonement shall be made on behalf of the Israelites for all their sins. And Moses did as the LORD had commanded him.

IV. Holiness Laws

17 **Sacredness of Blood.** ¹The LORD said to Moses: ²Speak to Aaron and his sons, as well as to all the Israelites, and tell them: This is what the LORD has commanded: ³Any Israelite who slaughters an ox or a sheep or a goat, whether in the camp or outside of it, ⁴without first bringing it to the entrance

---

In sum, blood purifies and re-consecrates the sacred space. The scapegoat takes away the sins of the people. This observance also involves fasting (literally, "afflicting the soul/spirit"), an ancient custom that was an act of piety as well as an expression of mourning or one's preparation to receive some divine revelation. In many Christian churches today the season of Lent is an annual time of fasting and penance, often associated with almsgiving and sharing the fruits of self-denial.

CODE OF LEGAL HOLINESS
Leviticus 17–26

The Holiness Code comprises a large block of laws enjoined on all the people, priests and laity alike. The reader should note that many of these laws take up matters that began in Leviticus 1–6 but now with more universal application. Unlike the laws regarding crime and civic duty found in Exodus and Deuteronomy, the Holiness Code focuses on religion and cult. As already noted, these liturgical laws find their theological foundation in the repeated call to holiness: "Be holy, for I, the LORD your God, am holy" (19:2; also 20:7, 26; 21:6, 8). In fact, reading chapter 19 first is a helpful way to become oriented to Leviticus 17–26 and the overall theological perspective of the Holiness Code.

17:1-16 Sacredness of blood

The chapter may be divided into two sections: verses 1-9 and 10-16. The first section relates to the slaughter of animals, and the second to the special treatment of blood. Both issues are intimately connected in the realm of the sacred. The narrative proceeds with a description of various circumstances

of the tent of meeting to present it as an offering to the LORD in front of the LORD's tabernacle, shall be judged guilty of bloodshed —that individual has shed blood, and shall be cut off from the people. ⁵This is so that such sacrifices as they used to offer in the open field the Israelites shall henceforth bring to the LORD at the entrance of the tent of meeting, to the priest, and sacrifice them there as communion sacrifices to the LORD. ⁶The priest will splash the blood on the altar of the LORD at the entrance of the tent of meeting and burn the fat for an odor pleasing to the LORD. ⁷No longer shall they offer their sacrifices to the demons with whom they prostituted themselves. This shall be an everlasting statute for them and their descendants.

⁸Tell them, therefore: Anyone, whether of the house of Israel or of the aliens residing among them, who offers a burnt offering or sacrifice ⁹without bringing it to the entrance of the tent of meeting to offer it to the LORD, shall be cut off from the people. ¹⁰As for anyone, whether of the house of Israel or of the aliens residing among them, who consumes any blood, I will set myself against that individual and will cut that person off from among the people, ¹¹since the life of the flesh is in the blood, and I have given it to you to make atonement on the altar for yourselves, because it is the blood as life that makes atonement. ¹²That is why I have told the Israelites: No one among you, not even a resident alien, may consume blood.

¹³Anyone hunting, whether of the Israelites or of the aliens residing among them, who catches an animal or a bird that may be eaten, shall pour out its blood and cover it with earth, ¹⁴since the ▶ life of all flesh is its blood. I have told the

(inside or outside the camp, Israelites or aliens in their midst, offerings destined for total sacrifice or eventually for table food). All animal sacrifice is regulated with an eye to communal and personal holiness. There is no provision for any "non-sacrificial" or secular slaughter of animals. The draining and burying of the blood, even of hunted animals for sport or food, speak most directly to this point (v. 13).

The discussion of blood in Leviticus 17 remains essential for our understanding of blood in the Scriptures. Blood is life and all animate creatures (animals and humans) have an inner component apart from the body but intimately related to it. A close reading of verse 11 helps our understanding of Old Testament anthropology: "the *life* of the *flesh* is in the *blood* . . ." (emphasis added). The life (Hebrew *nephesh*) refers to the spirit or spark of animation in a creature. It resides throughout life in the blood. The flesh (Hebrew *bāśār*) means a living being that grows, becomes old, dies, and returns to the dust of the earth. It is essentially the meat on the skeleton. The blood (Hebrew *dām*) is the seat of life in animate creatures. Its shedding depletes life and brings on death.

Israelites: You shall not consume the blood of any flesh. Since the life of all flesh is its blood, anyone who consumes it shall be cut off.

¹⁵Everyone, whether a native or an alien, who eats of an animal that died of itself or was killed by a wild beast, shall wash his garments, bathe in water, and be unclean until evening, and then become clean. ¹⁶If one does not wash his garments and bathe, that person shall bear the penalty.

18 Laws Concerning Sexual Behavior. ¹The LORD said to Moses:

²Speak to the Israelites and tell them: I, the LORD, am your God. ³You shall not do as they do in the land of Egypt, where you once lived, nor shall you do as they do in the land of Canaan, where I am bringing you; do not conform to their customs. ⁴My decrees you shall carry out, and my statutes you shall take care to follow. I, the LORD, am your God. ⁵Keep, then, my statutes and decrees, for the person who carries them out will find life through them. I am the LORD.

⁶None of you shall approach a close relative to have sexual intercourse. I am

---

These three components helped the ancients understand corporal life and death. This understanding is primitive by modern standards but bespeaks the perennial fascination with life, death, and the fragile mysteries of mortality. The modern reader must not confuse *nephesh* (spark of life, spirit, soul) with the Christian understanding of an immortal soul separate from the body. Those categories arose in later Greek philosophy (body vs. soul) and went on to inform Christian theology. The biblical meaning of the body is more holistic.

The end of chapter 17 addresses the eating of carrion or animals killed by other beasts. Animals that eat decaying flesh are already forbidden as food (ch. 11). By extension human consumption of animals found dead is forbidden. The ritual washing harks back to 11:25 and reiterates the uncleanness that can come from contact with the dead. Again, the issue is not sinfulness (burial requires human contact). Rather, ritual purification informs the meaning of such laws.

18:1-30 The sanctity of sexuality

Major issues surround the sanctity of sex: life and death, property and boundaries, rights and obligations, penalties for misconduct, and most importantly the tragedy of innocence lost and the violation of right relationships. Thus the Scriptures emphasize that all creation is sacred and answerable to God for the abuse of the gifts of life. Recent socio-cultural biblical criticism has informed our understanding of the ancient biblical world, including the rationale for many of the customs that were important in those times.

the LORD. [7]You shall not disgrace your father by having intercourse with your mother. She is your own mother; you shall not have intercourse with her. [8]You shall not have intercourse with your father's wife, for that would be a disgrace to your father. [9]You shall not have intercourse with your sister, your father's daughter or your mother's daughter, whether she was born in your own household or born elsewhere. [10]You shall not have intercourse with your son's daughter or with your daughter's daughter, for that would be a disgrace to you. [11]You shall not have intercourse with the daughter whom your father's wife bore to him in his household, since she, too, is your sister. [12]You shall not have intercourse with your father's sister, since she is your father's relative. [13]You shall not have intercourse with your mother's sister, since she is your mother's relative. [14]You shall not disgrace your father's brother by having sexual relations with his wife, since she, too, is your aunt. [15]You shall not have intercourse with your daughter-in-law; she is your son's wife; you shall not have intercourse with her. [16]You shall not have intercourse with your brother's wife; that would be a disgrace to your brother. [17]You shall not have intercourse with a woman and also with her daughter, nor shall you marry and have intercourse with her son's daughter or her daughter's daughter; they are related to her. This would be shameful. [18]While your wife is still living you shall not marry her sister as her rival and have intercourse with her.

[19]You shall not approach a woman to have intercourse with her while she is in her menstrual uncleanness. [20]You shall

To the modern reader some of these laws seem antiquated or are illegal in modern jurisprudence. Others seem universally correct and simply common sense. One must strive to distinguish between any particular practice and the morality behind it. For example, in ancient societies a girl of thirteen or so was of marriageable age, and degrees of separation (the marriage of cousins) were more proximate than many modern laws allow. Ancient marriages were normally arranged by families rather than by falling in love and announcing marriage to the family.

These perspectives inform the reader's thoughtful reading of Leviticus 18. One must not be immediately presumptive or judgmental, but rather ask what moral values ground a particular law. One must avoid the tendency to pick and choose based on one's own canons of morality. Such subjectivity is not helpful to understanding biblical texts. While condemning certain practices (e.g., brother-sister marriage, cultic prostitution, and child sacrifice), nowhere do the laws in Leviticus forbid intermarriage with other nations. That prohibition is extant, however, in other biblical laws (Exod 34:11-17; Deut 7:3-4). In sum, such differences demand a contextual reading of all biblical laws.

not have sexual relations with your neighbor's wife, defiling yourself with her. 21You shall not offer any of your offspring for immolation to Molech, thus profaning the name of your God. I am the LORD. 22You shall not lie with a male as with a woman; such a thing is an abomination. 23You shall not have sexual relations with an animal, defiling yourself with it; nor shall a woman set herself in front of an animal to mate with it; that is perverse.

24Do not defile yourselves by any of these things, because by them the nations whom I am driving out of your way have defiled themselves. 25And so the land has become defiled, and I have punished it for its wickedness, and the land has vomited out its inhabitants. 26You, however, must keep my statutes and decrees, avoiding all these abominations, both the natives and the aliens resident among you— 27because the previous inhabitants did all these abominations and the land became defiled; 28otherwise the land will vomit you out also for having defiled it, just as it vomited out the nations before you. 29For

---

In verses 1-18 the Egyptians and Canaanites serve as examples of practices abhorrent to Israel. The command not to serve other gods is repeated throughout this section (vv. 3 [twice], 24, 26, 27, 29, 30). Israelites must not conform to pagan customs, but no ban on intermarriage is stated. The laws begin with the closest degrees of kinship. Intercourse with blood relatives or those in the family by marriage is strictly forbidden. The repetition of "disgrace" (vv. 7-19; literally, "uncover the nakedness of") deserves comment. Intercourse with one's closest kin brings shame on the family, whether the act becomes known or not. Social justice is also involved. Widows must not become prey to sexual aggression or male opportunism at the death of a spouse.

Verses 19-23 begin with the prohibition of intercourse with a woman during menstruation or with another man's wife. Adultery is forbidden in the Ten Commandments (Exod 20:14; Deut 22:22), and Leviticus 20:10 imposes the death penalty for this offense. It is noteworthy that the laws of adultery were less strict for a male. A man committed adultery *against another man's marriage*; a woman committed adultery *with any man*. Hence, a married man's liaison with an unmarried woman, such as a prostitute, was not forbidden.

Child sacrifice to Molech (v. 21) refers to a Canaanite practice that was an abomination for ancient Israel. The name Molech occurs here and in 20:2-5. Sacrificing children is evidenced throughout Old Testament as a pagan ritual and, at times, crept into Israelite worship (cf. 2 Kgs 16:3 [Ahaz]). The primary motivation in verse 23 is the integrity of Israelite worship. The Lord is their God, whose name is profaned by calling on other gods.

whoever does any of these abominations shall be cut off from the people. ³⁰Heed my charge, then, not to observe the abominable customs that have been observed before your time, and thus become impure by them. I, the LORD, am your God.

19 **Various Rules of Conduct.** ¹The LORD said to Moses: ²Speak to the whole Israelite community and tell them: Be holy, for I, the LORD your God, am holy. ³Each of you revere your mother and father, and keep my sabbaths. I, the LORD, am your God.

As seen in previous sections, chapter 18 ends with a closing exhortation (vv. 24-30). This exhortation is more decisive than others so far, and the Lord speaks most personally and directly to all the people ("your" is plural): "I, the LORD, am *your* God" (v. 30; emphasis added). No ritual of purification is available to right a sexual abomination. The very land must be purged of sexual violence because life and blessing underlie the scriptural understanding of sexuality.

19:1-37 Various rules of conduct

The reader will notice that chapter 19 calls to mind the Ten Commandments and the two essential foci of all scriptural law: to God and to one's neighbor. Holiness is the primary theme here: be holy as the Lord is holy (19:2). The intrinsic nature of God (holiness) must inform human morality. Moral behavior is more than what seems right or serves good social order. The very actions of God observed in creation inform all human law, whether simple or complex. As the heavenly bodies and the seasons obey God's laws in creation, so must humankind (Gen 1; Job 38).

19:3 Revere parents and keep the sabbath

Respect for parents and elders was a primary value in ancient society, and certain laws impose a harsh penalty for insubordination (Deut 21:18-21 [stoning to death]). The wisdom literature offers the widest discussion of family values and raising children (Prov 3:11-12; 13:1; 31:28; Sir 3:1-16; 30:1-13). Many modern societies have an understanding of child development very different from the ancient world. While we may give consideration to age-appropriate behavior, the ancients saw children as untamed and gradually tamed by discipline.

Further, we must realize that respecting parents in the Old Testament speaks more directly to adult children. Revering father and mother in the Ten Commandments means not to abandon them in their old age. In nomadic society, the cultural root of many ancient laws, seniors may not be able to keep up with the caravan. Their children must not abandon them

⁴Do not turn aside to idols, nor make molten gods for yourselves. I, the LORD, am your God.

⁵When you sacrifice your communion sacrifice to the LORD, you shall sacrifice it so that it is acceptable on your behalf. ⁶It must be eaten on the day of your sacrifice or on the following day. Whatever is left over until the third day shall be burned in fire. ⁷If any of it is eaten on the third day, it will be a desecrated offering and not be accepted; ⁸whoever eats of it then shall bear the penalty for having profaned what is sacred to the LORD. Such a one shall be cut off from the people.

---

or neglect their needs. This basic understanding informs parental respect in later settled societies. As the book of Sirach notes, "My son, be steadfast in honoring your father; / do not grieve him as long as he lives" (3:12).

Sabbath rest harks back to Genesis 2:1-3 where God rests on the seventh day. The history of sabbath observance is complicated. The essence of this law is freeing people from endless work, making time for the rest and worship, and behaving as God behaves. Rest even for the land is an extension of the sabbath ideal (see 25:1-7).

19:4 Prohibition of idols

Some Christian groups cite this and related passages as evidence for the prohibition of any divine iconography. However, the prohibition of idols is more nuanced than that. The Israelites must not understand God as confined to a molten image and believe that whatever happens to the object happens to God. Statues have no magical power. Divine freedom knows no compromise, and the true image of God is the human person (Gen 1:26-27).

The reader need but look at Genesis 31:25-35 (Rachel's theft of her father's gods) to see that Israel's early history included some use of images, especially statues. Early Christianity evidences frescoes and statues, e.g., the iconography in catacombs and ancient Christian churches. Modern Christians who use sacred images and statues should explain that these objects do not confine God or saints. They represent artistically some image or attribute that fosters piety and prayer, much like a photograph evokes the memory of a person.

19:5-8 The acceptable communion sacrifice

This section continues the communion sacrifice discussed in chapters 3 and 7. Food offered to God and then left to spoil is a desecration, so the offering must be consumed before the third day. The number three has the symbolic value of completeness and wholeness. There are three sections of the sanctuary, three times for daily prayer, and Jonah is in the belly of the

"Do not reap the field to its very edge, but leave the gleanings for the poor and the alien" (Lev 19:9-10).

⁹When you reap the harvest of your land, you shall not be so thorough that you reap the field to its very edge, nor shall you gather the gleanings of your harvest. ¹⁰Likewise, you shall not pick your vineyard bare, nor gather up the grapes that have fallen. These things you shall leave for the poor and the alien. I, the LORD, am your God.

¹¹You shall not steal. You shall not deceive or speak falsely to one another. ¹²You shall not swear falsely by my name, thus profaning the name of your God. I am the LORD.

¹³You shall not exploit your neighbor. ▶ You shall not commit robbery. You shall not withhold overnight the wages of your laborer. ¹⁴You shall not insult the

---

fish for three days. Hence, three symbolically represents the completion of the offering in a timely manner.

19:9-10 Sharing the harvest

This law bespeaks care for the poor in ancient Israel (see 23:22; Deut 24:19-22). The compassion of Boaz for the widow Ruth returning from famine speaks eloquently to the spirit of these verses (Ruth 2). It is noteworthy that widow-orphan-alien was the sacred triad of the poor and disenfranchised in the Old Testament. The book of Deuteronomy speaks most directly to these persons as a sacred triad (10:18; 24:17; 27:19). Hence, care for the poor enjoys a foundational place in ancient Israelite law and social justice.

19:11-18 Duties to one's neighbor

Right conduct with one's neighbor demands social justice in every area of life. Injustice shows itself in theft, deception, false witness, and most powerfully in hatred and revenge. Hence, this section begins with representative behaviors and builds up to the basic attitudes that motivate such behavior. The ultimate motivation for social justice is love of neighbor as oneself, the great Golden Rule.

Verses 11-12 juxtapose four interrelated verbs that condemn "robbing" one's neighbor of something. To steal (Hebrew *gānab*) bespeaks more than property theft. It includes kidnapping as well, a crime that robs a person of rightful freedom. To deceive (Hebrew *kāhash*) connotes the withholding of relevant information that robs another of justice. To speak falsely (Hebrew *shāqar*) means to engage in deception and fraud, a designation given to false prophets in Israel (Jer 14:14; 23:25-27). To swear falsely (Hebrew *shābaʿ*) usurps the uncompromised testimony an oath demands, i.e., to tell the truth, the whole truth, and nothing but the truth. Swearing falsely offends God who stands as the ultimate judge and sentence-giver. To promote the wrongful sentencing of a person in the name of God (perjury) is a great blasphemy.

deaf, or put a stumbling block in front of the blind, but you shall fear your God. I am the LORD.

¹⁵You shall not act dishonestly in rendering judgment. Show neither partiality to the weak nor deference to the mighty, but judge your neighbor justly.

¹⁶You shall not go about spreading slander among your people; nor shall you stand by idly when your neighbor's life is at stake. I am the LORD.

¹⁷You shall not hate any of your kindred in your heart. Reprove your neighbor openly so that you do not incur sin

In sum, stealth in all its forms sins against God and the community. The moral decay caused by "robbing" another person of some right affects the community and is not lost from God's judgment, even when done in secret. This value was powerful in the ancient world. The modern reader must acknowledge that physical evidence and sworn testimony have guided forensic justice for most of human history. Tales of perjury and payoffs abounded (see Dan 13 [Susanna's virtue]). There were no lie detector machines, DNA testing, and video surveillance. The sworn word held sway.

Verses 13-14 continue the theme of social justice. One must not withhold rightful payments to another. That, too, is a form of oppression. The person intended in verse 13 may well be the day laborer who lives off wages hand to mouth. Such persons need the constant trickle of minimal income to feed the family (cf. Deut 24:14-15). Such constant need flows well into care for the disabled person. Their situation is likewise chronic. In ancient Israel disabilities were often considered the consequence of sin (Deut 28:29). The blind and other disabled persons were banned from priestly service (Lev 21:18) and at times barred from the temple (2 Sam 5:8), but charity toward them was still enjoined on all of Israel. Verse 14 probably reflects the ban of cruel practical jokes at the expense of a disabled person. Amid uninformed social perceptions and biased laws, care for the disabled is a holy responsibility. Jesus' healing ministry in the gospels bespeaks this value. He reaches out to those often shunned by society.

Verses 15-16 juxtapose the unfair legal decision and slander against a neighbor. It is noteworthy that in verse 15 the poor are paired not with the rich but with the mighty. Abuse of power, not wealth in itself, is the issue. Leniency out of pity has its place but should not be a key factor in legal decisions. Likewise, deference to those with power and influence compromises the equality of all persons that true justice demands. Verse 16 makes two points related to commission and omission. First, spreading gossip never serves the good. Such information is usually biased, and the victim is not there to make a defense. Second, standing idly before a person in danger is a sin of omission. This law

◀ because of that person. ¹⁸Take no revenge and cherish no grudge against your own people. You shall love your neighbor as yourself. I am the LORD.

¹⁹Keep my statutes: do not breed any of your domestic animals with others of a different species; do not sow a field of yours with two different kinds of seed;

---

probably embraces a variety of circumstances, everything from personal injury to capital punishment. In sum, social justice demands vigilance against sins of commission and omission, doing and failing to do.

Verses 17-18 contrast hatred and love. These feelings come from the "heart" (Hebrew *lēb, lēbāb*), which in Israelite thought was not merely the seat of emotion and sentiment but rather intellect, will, and understanding. Hence, intention and memory are involved. This is the first of three occurrences in Leviticus of the term "heart" (also 26:36, 41), a grand motif in the Old Testament, occurring some eight hundred times. The Great Commandment ("Hear, O Israel!") in Deuteronomy 6:4-9 includes loving the Lord with all one's heart. The psalms proclaim the heart as the place where the Lord sees one's inner self (Ps 44:22) and tests one's intentions (Ps 7:3).

More deeply, the call to love and not hate rests on the fact that vengeance ultimately belongs to God: "You know, LORD: / Remember me and take care of me, / avenge me on my persecutors" (Jer 15:15; cf. Ps 94:1). God must delegate vengeance to humans. This belief, rooted in Israelite law, finds an early expression in Moses' killing of the Egyptian taskmaster (Exod 2:11-14). Moses acts alone and apart from God's revealed laws. Though filled with righteous indignation, he emerges not as the hero but a fugitive from justice. Moses flees to Midian and there encounters the Lord at the burning bush. Only later, after the exodus and the events at Sinai, do divine laws emerge that govern the human taking of life. Vigilante justice in any age never bespeaks divine justice.

These verses culminate in what we call the Golden Rule: love your neighbor as yourself. Recalling that the motif of the heart bespeaks more than emotions, this command includes intentionality. One's attitudes, behaviors, and choices must bespeak love. We love God by observing the revealed commandments. We love our neighbor by acts of social justice in line with God's commandments.

19:19-37 Miscellaneous laws

The laws discussed in this section are random and unsystematic. Basically, the matters concern secondary human relationships and material possessions.

and do not put on a garment woven with two different kinds of thread.

²⁰If a man has sexual relations with a female slave who has been acquired by another man but has not yet been redeemed or given her freedom, an investigation shall be made. They shall not be put to death, because she has not been freed. ²¹The man shall bring to the entrance of the tent of meeting as his repa-ration to the LORD a ram as a reparation offering. ²²With the ram of the reparation offering the priest shall make atonement before the LORD for the wrong the man has committed, so that he will be forgiven for the wrong he has committed.

²³When you come into the land and plant any fruit tree there, first look upon its fruit as if it were uncircumcised. For three years, it shall be uncircumcised for

Verse 19 is curious and has occasioned a variety of explanations. Literally, taking care to breed animals within their species bespeaks harmony in creation. God made the beasts and humankind in their intended order and relationship with one another. Indiscriminate interbreeding bespeaks primordial chaos. This law may also be a metaphor for illicit human relationships. One must not intermarry indiscriminately and engage in unlawful unions.

The laws regarding farming and clothing are extensions of the basic principle here, i.e., one must not mix foreign things and blur proper distinctions or boundaries. It may be that the farming and clothing laws are rooted in practical wisdom. Farming two crops in the same plot sometimes results in a poor harvest as each competes for nutrients from the soil or one overtakes the other. Different threads in sewing can shrink and cause clothing to pucker when washed. Such folk wisdom shows metaphorically that some "mixtures" in life do not do well. Water and oil do not mix.

Verses 20-22 address the case of a female slave betrothed to one man and seduced by another. Because the woman is property, her seducer atones with a simple offering. In terms of social justice, this violation bespeaks an abuse of the powerless. Such a violation is clearly against the Ten Commandments (Exod 20:17; Deut 5:21). This law seems out of place. Some suggest that it belongs after 20:12. For more on slave laws see Exodus 21:7-11.

Verses 23-25 discuss laws regarding fruit-bearing trees. The details indicate an appreciable knowledge of horticulture in the ancient world. Young fruit trees are left to bear unpicked fruit until the fourth year and such early fruit is metaphorically "uncircumcised." The fourth year crop is like a firstborn gift to the Lord and offered in the sanctuary. People can begin eating the fruit of the tree in the fifth year. This practice bespeaks the value of waiting and anticipation. Gifts of the earth take time, patience, and

you; it may not be eaten. ²⁴In the fourth year, however, all of its fruit shall be dedicated to the LORD in joyous celebration. ²⁵Not until the fifth year may you eat its fruit, to increase the yield for you. I, the LORD, am your God.

²⁶Do not eat anything with the blood still in it. Do not recite charms or practice soothsaying. ²⁷Do not clip your hair at the temples, nor spoil the edges of your beard. ²⁸Do not lacerate your bodies for the dead, and do not tattoo yourselves. I am the LORD.

²⁹You shall not degrade your daughter by making a prostitute of her; otherwise the land will prostitute itself and become full of lewdness. ³⁰Keep my sabbaths, and reverence my sanctuary. I am the LORD.

³¹Do not turn to ghosts or consult spirits, by which you will be defiled. I, the LORD, am your God.

---

skilled handling. The time it takes to enjoy eventually the grain, wine, and oil in their proper seasons relates to practical folk wisdom. As Ecclesiastes notes, "There is an appointed time for everything, / and a time for every affair under the heavens / . . . a time to plant, and a time to uproot the plant" (3:1-2).

Verses 26-28 address random pagan practices foreign to genuine Israelite worship. The practices in and of themselves are not the focus here. Rather, it is the presumed magical power or benefit therein that is condemned. In some ancient societies the hair represented the unique life force of an individual. Its color and shape bespoke one's personal uniqueness and, like bones and teeth, remained more or less intact after other body parts deteriorated. Hairstyles could represent a special office, which is much behind the grooming of the priest cited later in 21:5-6. He must not clip the crown of the head or spoil the edges of his beard. The same goes for lacerating himself. The pagans would lacerate themselves to get the gods' attention (1 Kgs 18:25-29 [the prophets of Baal]). Incised markings, piercing, and branding were methods of marking slaves (Exod 21:6; Deut 15:17).

Verse 29 speaks of prostitution, a practice not in itself prohibited in ancient Israelite law. Adultery is a separate matter because it violates a man's marriage. To degrade one's daughter in such a manner for profit is an abomination. It affects the very fabric of the family and social order.

Verse 30 reminds the reader that the sabbath is holy and its observance a way to holiness. A time of rest gives the people an opportunity to worship and is rooted in God's plan of creation (Gen 2:2-3).

Verse 31 resumes verses 26-28 and the rejection of certain pagan practices. To consult the dead via fortune-tellers and other mediums was a way of seeing into the future and perhaps manipulating one's fate. Such

³²Stand up in the presence of the aged, show respect for the old, and fear your God. I am the Lord.

³³When an alien resides with you in your land, do not mistreat such a one. ³⁴You shall treat the alien who resides with you no differently than the natives born among you; you shall love the alien as yourself; for you too were once aliens in the land of Egypt. I, the Lord, am your God.

³⁵Do not act dishonestly in using measures of length or weight or capacity. ³⁶You shall have a true scale and true weights, an honest ephah and an honest hin. I, the Lord, am your God, who brought you out of the land of Egypt. ³⁷Be careful, then, to observe all my statutes and decrees. I am the Lord.

20 **Penalties for Various Sins.** ¹The Lord said to Moses: ²Tell the Israelites: Anyone, whether an Israelite or

superstition, though evidenced in ancient Israel (Isa 8:19-20), is censured here and elsewhere (20:6, 20; Deut 18:10-12).

Verse 32 resumes the spirit of respect for the disabled enjoined in verse 14. Reverence of parents and elders stems from the Ten Commandments and finds its fullest expression in the Old Testament wisdom literature. Proverbs and Sirach discuss this theme in various places (Prov 10:1; 23:22-25; Sir 3:1-16).

Verses 33-34 remind the Israelites to care for the alien in their midst out of the remembrance that they were once themselves slaves in Egypt. This law echoes the spirit of Exodus 22:20 where care of the disenfranchised triad of widow-orphan-alien is motivated by the memory of the slavery of the Hebrews (also Exod 23:9; Deut 10:17-19; 24:17-18).

Verses 35-37 speak of justice in the marketplace, with verse 37 summing up the chapter. The term used to express dishonesty (Hebrew *ʿāwel*) bespeaks an unjust and sinful deed, not merely shady business practices to be winked at. Cheating in weights and balances was typical in the ancient world, so customers regularly bargained with vendors. The ephah was approximately six gallons and the hin one gallon, so the law concerns bulk sales.

The prophets (Hos 12:8; Amos 8:5; Mic 6:10-11) and the wisdom literature (Prov 11:1; 16:11; 20:10) railed against such dishonesty. The sin was most heinous when done against the poor and those with limited income (Amos 8:4).

20:1-27 The death penalty for the integrity of the land

This chapter contains various laws divided into two sections: the penalty of death (vv. 1-21, 27) and the integrity of the land (vv. 22-26). "Shall be put to death" is repeated through these laws and forms an *inclusio* for the chapter (vv. 2, 27). Certain sins are so heinous that the sinner must be

an alien residing in Israel, who gives offspring to Molech shall be put to death. The people of the land shall stone that person. ³I myself will turn against and cut off that individual from among the people; for in the giving of offspring to Molech, my sanctuary was defiled and my holy name was profaned. ⁴If the people of the land condone the giving of offspring to Molech, by failing to put the wrongdoer to death, ⁵I myself will turn against that individual and his or her family, and I will cut off from their people both the wrongdoer and all who follow this person by prostituting themselves with Molech.

⁶Should anyone turn to ghosts and spirits and prostitute oneself with them, I will turn against that person and cut such a one off from among the people. ⁷Sanctify yourselves, then, and be holy; for I, the LORD, your God, am holy. ⁸Be careful, therefore, to observe my statutes. I, the LORD, make you holy.

⁹Anyone who curses father or mother shall be put to death; and having cursed father or mother, such a one will bear the bloodguilt. ¹⁰If a man commits adultery with his neighbor's wife, both the adulterer and the adulteress shall be put to death. ¹¹If a man disgraces his father by lying with his father's wife, the two of

---

blotted out from the community, and the community members exact the execution. The term "people of the land" (Hebrew *ꜥam hāʾāres*) means "fellow citizens" here. These are probably the adult males who represent the community in the act of stoning, along with any formal witnesses against the person. Their act bespeaks a communal punishment that typically takes place outside the city (24:14).

Such violence seems harsh to the modern reader, but to the ancients the integrity of the land and the community superseded the individual. To their mind much was at stake with some sins, and the community good must take precedence. The stoning of Stephen in the New Testament indicates the gravity of the charges laid against him by his accusers. In their eyes he blasphemed the Mosaic law, the temple, and the stature of Moses (Acts 6:8-15).

20:1-21, 27 The death penalty

Similar laws are evidenced elsewhere in the Old Testament. Murder (Gen 9:6; Exod 21:12), adultery (Deut 22:20-21), kidnapping (Exod 21:16), and even striking parents (Exod 21:15) called for capital punishment. Stoning and burning were the most typical forms of execution.

Verses 2-5 discuss an abomination that combines murder and idolatry. The Lord will notice and punish attempts to abet or cover up child sacrifice. The fourfold repetition of Molech, a pagan god associated with human sacrifice, contextualizes the ban. The details of this prohibition are telling. Sacrificing one's offspring is rooted in the idea that returning "first fruits"

them shall be put to death; their bloodguilt is upon them. ¹²If a man lies with his daughter-in-law, both of them shall be put to death; they have done what is perverse; their bloodguilt is upon them. ¹³If a man lies with a male as with a woman, they have committed an abomination; the two of them shall be put to death; their bloodguilt is upon them. ¹⁴If a man marries a woman and her mother also, that is shameful conduct; the man and the two women as well shall be burned to death, so that shamefulness may not be found among you. ¹⁵If a man has sexual relations with an animal, the man shall be put to death, and you shall kill the animal. ¹⁶If a woman goes up to any animal to mate with it, you shall kill the woman and the animal; they shall both be put to death;

---

to the gods would assure fertility in the future. While acknowledging that the first male offspring belonged to God (Exod 22:29-30), Israelite law called for a substitute animal offering (Exod 13:12-13; Num 18:15). Further, such an abominable sacrifice defiles the sanctuary. The Lord is intrinsically holy, so such a practice is impure and desecrating by its very nature. At times ancient Israel dappled in such pagan practices, but authentic worship demanded allegiance to the Lord.

Verse 6 condemns the consultation of mediums and fortune-tellers. Such persons engage in necromancy, i.e., the consultation of ghosts to learn secrets of the future. The secrets allow someone to know the future in advance or try to alter the intended future. The manipulative nature of such superstitions is foreign to divine freedom and human openness to the will of God.

Verses 7-8 again exhort holiness, the quality that sets authentic worship apart from pagan superstitions and practices. Obedience is a way to holiness, and God shows holiness in mighty deeds that evoke awe and reverence.

Verses 9-21 list numerous acts that bring disgrace on the family. Any one of these acts breaks the fabric of familial and communal integrity. Parental disrespect heads the list. The modern reader may find the death penalty harsh, but the foundational importance of father and mother underlies this teaching. All other family relations stand on honor of parents as one's human creators and first teachers.

Sexual misconduct violates another man's property (spouse, children, slaves, animals), but more profoundly tears at the fabric of the household and the extended family (cf. 18:1-18). The abuse of power is also involved. Sexuality is a strong symbol of human power used to humiliate, subjugate, and steal from others, both physically and emotionally. Leviticus demands the harshest of penalties.

their bloodguilt is upon them. [17]If a man marries his sister, his father's daughter or his mother's daughter, and they have intercourse with each other, that is disgraceful; they shall be publicly cut off from the people; the man shall bear the penalty of having had intercourse with his own sister. [18]If a man lies with a woman during her menstrual period and has intercourse with her, he has laid bare the source of her flow and she has uncovered it. The two of them shall be cut off from the people. [19]You shall not have intercourse with your mother's sister or your father's sister, because that dishonors one's own flesh; they shall bear their penalty. [20]If a man lies with his uncle's wife, he disgraces his uncle; they shall bear the penalty; they shall die childless. [21]If a man takes his brother's wife, it is severe defilement and he has disgraced his brother; they shall be childless.

[22]Be careful to observe all my statutes and all my decrees; otherwise the land where I am bringing you to dwell will vomit you out. [23]Do not conform, there-

---

Verse 27 picks up on verse 6 and further condemns those who act as mediums and fortune-tellers. Its position is awkward in the flow of the narrative, but it does add an element of personal responsibility for engaging in superstitions. The verse sums up all the laws in the chapter: "their bloodguilt is upon them."

20:22-26 The integrity of the land

These five verses form a smoother end to the chapter if verse 27 is read immediately after verse 6. The fourfold repetition of "land" or "ground" (Hebrew *ʾeres* or *ʾădāmâ* [each twice]) punctuates this section, as well as the twofold repetition of holiness (Hebrew *qādôsh*). The land and its people must be holy as God is holy. The land is a gift the Lord is bringing them to, not a land they earn for themselves (vv. 22, 24). Therein, the Israelites must distinguish and separate the clean from the unclean, a command that harks back to 10:10 and 11:47. The Israelites themselves are a people set apart.

Leviticus 18–20 forms a splendid unit in its own right. Though many of its laws are time conditioned, the content demonstrates that ancient Israel and many neighboring cultures valued social harmony and ethical human relationships. The Golden Rule in 19:18 succinctly teaches that charity and justice bespeak fidelity to God. This rule also affirms that ritual sacrifice without the proper inner disposition is empty. The same spirit governs the New Testament. In Jesus' warning against anger he admonishes the crowd to leave their gifts at the altar if there is need of reconciliation (Matt 5:21-26). The letter of James affirms that faith and good works go hand in hand (2:14-26).

fore, to the customs of the nations whom I am driving out of your way, because all these things that they have done have filled me with disgust for them. ²⁴But to you I have said: You shall take possession of their land. I am giving it to you to possess, a land flowing with milk and honey. I, the LORD, am your God, who have set you apart from other peoples. ²⁵You, too, must set apart, then, the clean animals from the unclean, and the clean birds from the unclean, so that you do not make yourselves detestable through any beast or bird or any creature which creeps on the ground that I have set apart for you as unclean. ²⁶To me, therefore, you shall be holy; for I, the LORD, am holy, and I have set you apart from other peoples to be my own.

²⁷A man or a woman who acts as a medium or clairvoyant shall be put to death. They shall be stoned to death; their bloodguilt is upon them.

21 **Sanctity of the Priesthood.** ¹The LORD said to Moses: Speak to the priests, Aaron's sons, and tell them: None of you shall make himself unclean for any dead person among his kindred, ²except for his nearest relatives, his mother or father, his son or daughter, his brother ³or his unmarried sister, who is of his own family while she remains single; for these he may make himself unclean. ⁴But as a husband among his kindred he shall not make himself unclean and thus profane himself.

⁵The priests shall not make bald the crown of their head, nor shave the edges of their beard, nor lacerate their body. ⁶They shall be holy to their God, and shall not profane their God's name, since they offer the oblations of the LORD, the food of their God; so they must be holy.

⁷A priest shall not marry a woman debased by prostitution, nor a woman who has been divorced by her husband; for the priest is holy to his God. ⁸Honor him as holy for he offers the food of your God; he shall be holy to you, because I, the LORD, am holy who make you holy.

21:1-15 Sanctity of the priesthood

Though priesthood and priestly duties are discussed earlier in Leviticus, the subject gets its most focused attention here. The priest, set apart to mediate and officiate for the people, must embody distinct qualities and a particular lifestyle. First, he must not touch the dead except for the burial preparation of nearest relatives. This taboo extends from his duty to distinguish between the clean and unclean (10:10) and to act as guardian of the sanctuary.

Second, he must keep laws regarding shaving the head or beard, which are related to ancient mourning practices. The same applies to self-laceration (cf. 19:27-28). His ministry centers in the sanctuary and its environs, so he must not become ritually defiled or appear bodily unkempt. The modern reader must remember that the dead were not brought into the temple for a memorial service but buried with dispatch. Different customs of mourning and burial apply to biblical texts.

⁹If a priest's daughter debases herself by prostitution, she thereby debases her father; she shall be burned with fire.

¹⁰The most exalted of the priests, upon whose head the anointing oil has been poured and who has been ordained to wear the special vestments, shall not dishevel his hair or rend his garments, ¹¹nor shall he go near any dead person. Not even for his father or mother may he thus become unclean; ¹²nor shall he leave the sanctuary and profane the sanctuary of his God, for the consecration of the anointing oil of his God is upon him. I am the Lord.

¹³He shall marry only a woman who is a virgin. ¹⁴He shall not marry a widow or a woman who has been divorced or one who has been debased by prostitution, but only a virgin, taken from his kindred, he shall marry, ¹⁵so that he not profane his offspring among his kindred. I, the Lord, make him holy.

Priestly Blemishes. ¹⁶The Lord said to Moses: ¹⁷Say to Aaron: None of your descendants, throughout their generations, who has any blemish shall come forward to offer the food of his God. ¹⁸Anyone who has any of the following blemishes may not come forward: he

---

The sanctity of the priests demands that they marry only women of pure lineage. The bride could not be a prostitute or any non-virgin, even if the previous victim of rape. The daughter of a priest incurs the harshest of penalties for shaming her lineage. The death penalty indicates that any sexual misconduct of the priest's children, even a consensual act, was more heinous than with commoners.

Verses 10-12 relate to the high priest, literally, "the priest who is exalted above his fellows." He is anointed on the head, while the other priests' clothing is anointed (see 8:30). The application of oil and special vestments bespeaks his consecration and mandate to fulfill his duties as high priest.

Verses 13-15 complement verses 7-8, adding to the list of unqualified brides for the priest. Virginity is the issue, not the character of the woman. One should recall that a widow could face economic hardship if her deceased husband's family disowned her and she was unable to reunite with her family.

21:16-24 Priestly blemishes

Defects were prohibited on all beings associated with sacrifices, human and beast alike (cf. 22:19-25). However, a priest with a bodily defect could serve in areas not associated with the altar, the place "to offer the food of his God" (v. 17). In the ancient world deformities were often considered signs of divine punishment for personal sin or that of one's ancestors. The book of Job uses being without defect as a metaphor for moral living (11:15; 31:7; see also Prov 9:7), and the New Testament draws on such imagery to describe Jesus as the unblemished Lamb of God (Heb 9:14; 1 Pet 1:19).

who is blind, or lame, or who has a split lip, or a limb too long, [19]or a broken leg or arm, [20]or who is a hunchback or dwarf or has a growth in the eye, or who is afflicted with sores, scabs, or crushed testicles. [21]No descendant of Aaron the priest who has any such blemish may draw near to offer the oblations of the LORD; on account of his blemish he may not draw near to offer the food of his God. [22]He may, however, eat the food of his God: of the most sacred as well as sacred offerings. [23]Only, he may not enter through the veil nor draw near to the altar on account of his blemish; he shall not profane my sacred precincts, for it is I, the LORD, who make them holy.

[24]Moses, therefore, told this to Aaron and his sons and to all the Israelites.

22 Priestly Purity. [1]The LORD said to Moses: [2]Tell Aaron and his sons to treat with respect the sacred offerings which the Israelites consecrate to me; otherwise they will profane my holy name. I am the LORD.

[3]Tell them: If any one of you, or of your descendants in any future generation, dares, while he is in a state of uncleanness, to draw near the sacred offerings which the Israelites consecrate

to the LORD, such a one shall be cut off from my presence. I am the LORD.

[4]No descendant of Aaron who is stricken with a scaly infection, or who suffers from a genital discharge, may eat of the sacred offerings, until he again becomes clean. Moreover, if anyone touches a person who has become unclean by contact with a corpse, or if anyone has had an emission of semen, [5]or if anyone touches any swarming creature whose uncleanness is contagious or any person whose uncleanness, of whatever kind it may be, is contagious—[6]the one who touches such as these shall be unclean until evening and may not eat of the sacred portions until he has first bathed his body in water. [7]Then, when the sun sets, he shall be clean. Only then may he eat of the sacred offerings, for they are his food. [8]He shall not make himself unclean by eating of any animal that has died of itself or has been killed by wild beasts. I am the LORD.

[9]They shall keep my charge so that they will not bear the punishment in this matter and die for their profanation. I am the LORD who makes them holy.

[10]Neither an unauthorized person nor a priest's tenant or laborer may eat of any sacred offering. [11]But a slave

---

22:1-16 Priestly purity

The impurities in verses 4-9 hark back to sections in chapters 13–15. Intentionality distinguishes the cases cited here. Intentional sin merits being cut off from the Lord and the community (v. 3). Unintentional impurity renders a person unclean for a period of time (v. 4).

Lay persons become the focus in verses 10-16. Those in some relationship with the priest (his slaves and their children, his hired laborers, or a daughter returned to his house) may partake of the sacrificial food. Those with no such status are excluded.

whom a priest acquires by purchase or who is born in his house may eat of his food. ¹²A priest's daughter who is married to an unauthorized person may not eat of the sacred contributions. ¹³But if a priest's daughter is widowed or divorced and, having no children, returns to her father's house, she may then eat of her father's food as in her youth. No unauthorized person, however, may eat of it. ¹⁴If such a one eats of a sacred offering through inadvertence, that person shall make restitution to the priest for the sacred offering, with an increment of one fifth of the amount. ¹⁵The priests shall not allow the sacred offerings which the Israelites contribute to the LORD to be profaned ¹⁶nor make them incur a penalty when they eat their sacred offerings. For I, the LORD, make them holy.

Unacceptable Victims. ¹⁷The LORD said to Moses: ¹⁸Speak to Aaron and his sons and to all the Israelites, and tell them: When anyone of the house of Israel, or any alien residing in Israel, who presents an offering, brings a burnt offering as a votive offering or as a voluntary offering to the LORD, ¹⁹if it is to be acceptable for you, it must be an unblemished male of the herd, of the sheep or of the goats. ²⁰You shall not offer one that has any blemish, for such a one would not be acceptable on your behalf. ²¹When anyone presents a communion sacrifice to the LORD from the herd or the flock in fulfillment of a vow, or as a voluntary offering, if it is to find acceptance, it must be unblemished; it shall not have any blemish. ²²One that is blind or lame or maimed, or one that has running lesions or sores or scabs, you shall not offer to the LORD; do not put such an animal on the altar as an oblation to the LORD. ²³An ox or a sheep that has a leg that is too long or is stunted you may indeed present as a voluntary offering, but it will not be acceptable as a votive offering. ²⁴One that has its testicles bruised or crushed or torn out or cut off you shall not offer to the LORD. You shall neither do this in your own land ²⁵nor receive from a foreigner any such animals to offer up as the food of your God; since they are deformed or blemished, they will not be acceptable on your behalf.

²⁶The LORD said to Moses: ²⁷When an ox or a lamb or a goat is born, it shall

22:17-30 Unacceptable victims

As the priest must be unblemished, so must the sacrificial animal. Certain blemishes are easily recognizable and make for immediate rejection; other defects are minor and acceptable for a free-will offering but not a votive offering (22:23). Minor defects include the stunted growth of an otherwise healthy animal. Waiting until the eighth day to take a sacrificial animal from its mother bespeaks the spirit of the seven days: a symbolic value associated with rest, completion, and a parallel with the seven-day creation schema in Genesis 1. This waiting period also calls to mind the octave of ordination discussed in chapter 9. Timing is often significant in these laws.

remain with its mother for seven days; only from the eighth day onward will it be acceptable, to be offered as an oblation to the LORD. ²⁸You shall not slaughter an ox or a sheep on one and the same day with its young. ²⁹Whenever you offer a thanksgiving sacrifice to the LORD, so offer it that it may be acceptable on your behalf; ³⁰it must be eaten on the same day; none of it shall be left over until morning. I am the LORD.

³¹Be careful to observe my commandments. I am the LORD. ³²Do not profane my holy name, that in the midst of the Israelites I may be hallowed. I, the LORD, make you holy, ³³who led you out of the land of Egypt to be your God. I am the LORD.

23 **Holy Days.** ¹The LORD said to Moses: ²Speak to the Israelites and tell them: The following are the festivals of the LORD, which you shall declare holy days. These are my festivals:

³For six days work may be done; but the seventh day is a sabbath of complete rest, a declared holy day; you shall do

---

22:31-33 A closing exhortation

These verses are punctuated with the call to holiness. The profane is incompatible with the sacred, and the true Israelite must make a choice. God's intrinsic holiness remains the standard of all human choices. When one brings a sacrifice to the altar, the holy name of God is invoked. This gesture joins the grain or animal sacrifice to God. The memory of slavery in Egypt remains a timeless reason for observing the commandments and is repeated throughout the Old Testament.

23:1-44 Holy days

Communal celebrations through the liturgical year give identity and order to the religious community. Hence, the emphasis on second-person *plural* pronouns and verbs in this section highlights the communal nature of the laws enjoined. Spring and fall festivals, three in each season, characterize the worship calendar of ancient Israel. In the spring season Passover and Unleavened Bread (vv. 4-8), First Fruits (vv. 9-14), and Pentecost (vv. 15-22, also called Weeks) occur. In the fall the New Year (vv. 23-25), the Day of Atonement (vv. 26-32), and Booths (vv. 33-44, also called Succoth) take place. Woven through these annual feasts is the weekly sabbath observance (v. 3).

It is noteworthy that the sabbath observance is enjoined on the Israelites as a people (v. 2), not the priests as its presider. The laity has the primary responsibility for regular sabbath observance through the weeks of the year. This observance is rooted in creation where God enjoins humankind to be vigilant of the days and years (Gen 1:14) and to rest as God rests (Gen 2:3). Sabbath recurs weekly in the calendar; the other celebrations are moveable feasts in their proper season.

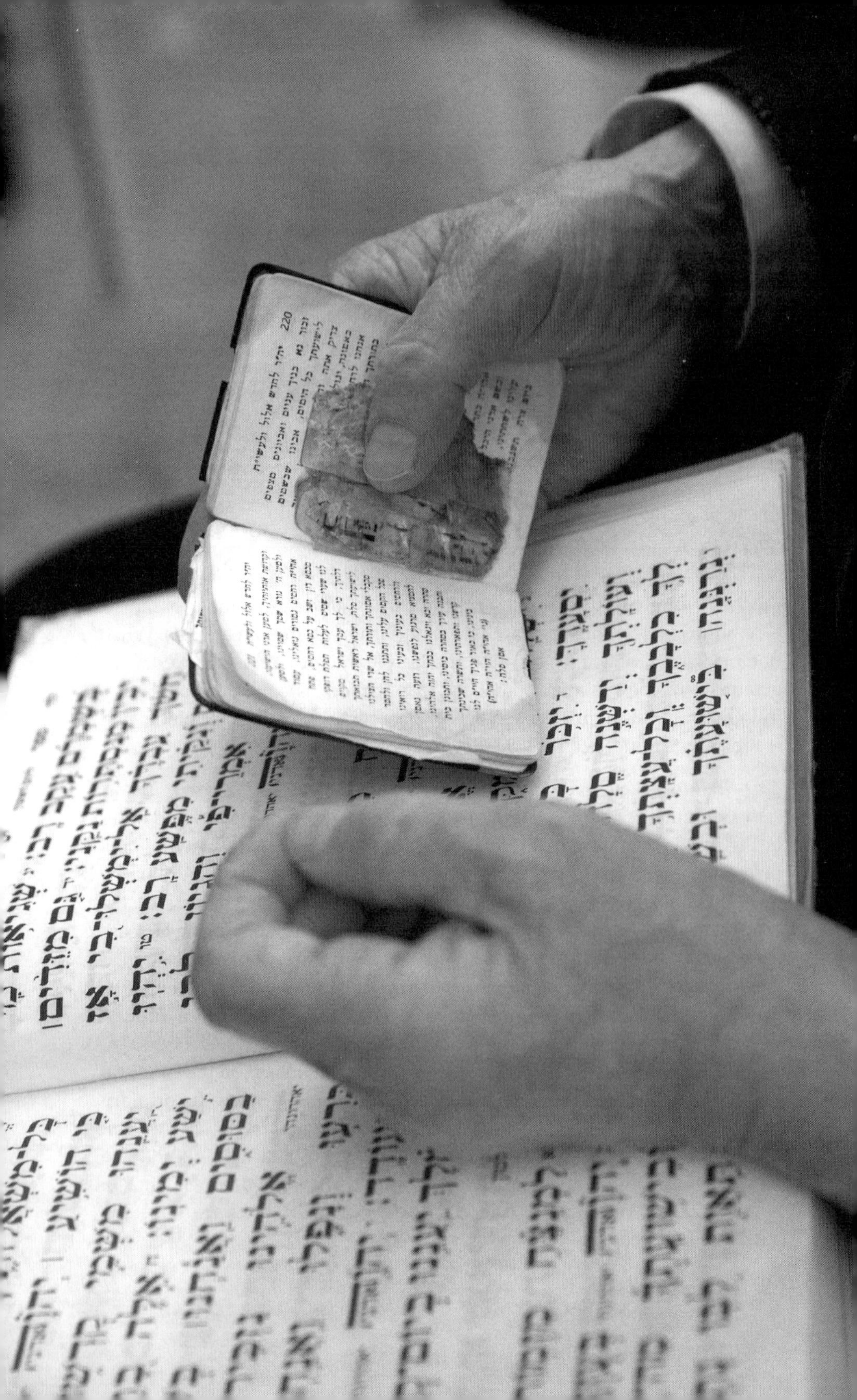
220

no work. It is the LORD's sabbath wherever you dwell.

Passover. ⁴These are the festivals of the LORD, holy days which you shall declare at their proper time. ⁵The Passover of the LORD falls on the fourteenth day of the first month, at the evening twilight. ⁶The fifteenth day of this month is the LORD's feast of Unleavened Bread. For seven days you shall eat unleavened bread. ⁷On the first of these days you will have a declared holy day; you shall do no heavy work. ⁸On each of the seven days you shall offer an oblation to the LORD. Then on the seventh day you will have a declared holy day; you shall do no heavy work.

⁹The LORD said to Moses: ¹⁰Speak to the Israelites and tell them: When you come into the land which I am giving you, and reap its harvest, you shall bring the first sheaf of your harvest to the

---

23:1-3 The sabbath

This observance sets a weekly day of rest and mirrors God's rest after creation: "On the seventh day God completed the work he had been doing; he rested on the seventh day from all the work he had undertaken. God blessed the seventh day and made it holy . . ." (Gen 2:2-3). God is intrinsically holy, so what better way to emulate that holiness than to act as God does. Sabbath imitates the cycle and rhythm of creation, that order that God brought out of chaos. Sabbath is for everyone: free persons, slaves, and even the animals.

23:4-14 Passover and Unleavened Bread

These feasts are discussed more fully in Exodus 12:1-20 and Numbers 28:17-25. They were originally separate festivals celebrating the first fruits of the harvest: the Passover of the shepherd and his flocks, the Unleavened Bread of the farmer and his crops. Once combined, they celebrate the memory of freedom from slavery in Egypt and the exodus journey (Exod 1–15, especially chs. 12–13).

First sheaves or fruits (vv. 9-14) celebrate the barley harvest. Barley is planted in the fall/winter season and reaped in the spring. This grain is generally heartier than wheat and can grow in less than ideal soil. This quality lends to the grain's inclusion in the list of produce that symbolizes blessings for Israel in the Promised Land (Deut 8:8). The elevation of the sheaf expresses thanks in the present and prayers for continued abundance in the future.

The theology of remembering and retelling informs the meaning of this festival: "When your children ask you, 'What does this rite of yours mean?' you will reply, 'It is the Passover sacrifice for the LORD, who passed over the houses of the Israelites in Egypt; when he struck down the Egyptians, he

priest, [11]who shall elevate the sheaf before the Lord that it may be acceptable on your behalf. On the day after the sabbath the priest shall do this. [12]On this day, when your sheaf is elevated, you shall offer to the Lord for a burnt offering an unblemished yearling lamb. [13]Its grain offering shall be two tenths of an ephah of bran flour mixed with oil, as a sweet-smelling oblation to the Lord; and its libation shall be a fourth of a hin of wine. [14]You shall not eat any bread or roasted grain or fresh kernels until this day, when you bring the offering for your God. This shall be a perpetual statute throughout your generations wherever you dwell.

Pentecost. [15]Beginning with the day after the sabbath, the day on which you bring the sheaf for elevation, you shall count seven full weeks; [16]you shall count to the day after the seventh week, fifty days. Then you shall present a new grain offering to the Lord. [17]For the elevated offering of your first-ripened fruits to the Lord, you shall bring with you from wherever you live two loaves of bread

---

delivered our houses'" (Exod 12:26-27). To remember these saving events is not simply a recollection of the past. By sharing in this family meal the participants become exodus people in the present.

The history of Passover is rich and complex. A family celebration in its origins, it later becomes a pilgrimage festival to Jerusalem (Deut 16:1-8). Today the Jewish Passover Haggadah (Sedar Meal) continues this annual festival. Appreciation of Passover theology also informs our understanding of the Eucharist in the church. The gospels place Jesus' death at the time of Passover and Unleavened Bread (e.g., Mark 14:12-15), and Paul uses these feasts in exhorting Christians to moral living (1 Cor 5:6-8).

23:15-22 Pentecost

Also called Weeks, this feast celebrates the first wheat harvest and occurs seven weeks after Passover and Unleavened Bread (hence Pentecost or "fiftieth"). Bread from the wheat harvest, several sacrificial animals, and libations are included (vv. 18-19). The libation is typically wine poured on the altar. The association of wine with festivities offers a vivid metaphor for ritual abuses and dappling in paganism: "Indeed, you poured out a drink offering to them, / and brought up grain offerings. / With these things, should I be appeased?" (Isa 57:6).

As with Passover and Unleavened Bread, Pentecost later became a pilgrimage feast (Deut 16:9-12). Its origins are in the farmer bringing first fruits of the harvest to a local shrine. In the postexilic period (Second Temple Judaism) the association with agriculture waned and the feast became associated with the making of the Sinai covenant, based on its timing in the spring (see Exod 19:1; 2 Chr 15:8-15).

made of two tenths of an ephah of bran flour and baked with leaven. [18]Besides the bread, you shall offer to the LORD a burnt offering of seven unblemished yearling lambs, one bull of the herd, and two rams, along with their grain offering and libations, as a sweet-smelling oblation to the LORD. [19]One male goat shall be sacrificed as a purification offering, and two yearling lambs as a communion sacrifice. [20]The priest shall elevate them—that is, the two lambs—with the bread of the first-ripened fruits as an elevated offering before the LORD; these shall be sacred to the LORD and belong to the priest. [21]On this same day you shall make a proclamation: there shall be a declared holy day for you; no heavy work may be done. This shall be a per-petual statute through all your genera-tions wherever you dwell.

[22]When you reap the harvest of your land, you shall not be so thorough that you reap the field to its very edge, nor shall you gather the gleanings of your harvest. These things you shall leave for the poor and the alien. I, the LORD, am your God.

New Year's Day. [23]The LORD said to Moses: [24]Tell the Israelites: On the first day of the seventh month you will have a sabbath rest, with trumpet blasts as a reminder, a declared holy day; [25]you shall do no heavy work, and you shall offer an oblation to the LORD.

The Day of Atonement. [26]The LORD said to Moses: [27]Now the tenth day of this seventh month is the Day of Atonement.

Verse 22 echoes the spirit of the second harvest (19:9-10). Amid all its ritual laws, Leviticus repeatedly enjoins the care of the poor. The repetition of this law reminds the hearer that charity is an ongoing obligation through-out the year and not a seasonal time of almsgiving. Such charity is grounded in that fact that the Lord demands it: "I, the LORD, am your God."

23:23-25 The New Year

Leviticus now moves to the autumn feasts on the calendar. New Year was the time of celebration and renewal. Ancient societies record a myriad of New Year rites, including parading statues of the gods and holding lavish banquets. The trumpet blasts were festive accents rooted in calling on the gods' attention to ongoing fertility, including abundant rainfall and productive flocks and crops. People made wishes for the coming year, believing at the same time that the gods were setting their destinies. New Year also invites attention to remembering what God has wrought for the people. This point harks back to the theology of remembering in Passover and Unleavened Bread (vv. 4-14).

23:26-32 The Day of Atonement

The Day of Atonement caps off the fall festivals that begin with New Year (see ch. 16). This is a time of introspection, penance, and prayer. It has a certain sabbath character to it: a ritual retreat from the routine of daily life.

You will have a declared holy day. You shall humble yourselves and offer an oblation to the LORD. ²⁸On this day you shall not do any work, because it is the Day of Atonement, when atonement is made for you before the LORD, your God. ²⁹Those who do not humble themselves on this day shall be cut off from the people. ³⁰If anyone does any work on this day, I will remove that person from the midst of the people. ³¹You shall do no work; this is a perpetual statute throughout your generations wherever you dwell; ³²it is a sabbath of complete rest for you. You shall humble yourselves. Beginning on the evening of the ninth of the month, you shall keep your sabbath from evening to evening.

The Feast of Booths. ³³The LORD said to Moses: ³⁴Tell the Israelites: The fifteenth day of this seventh month is the LORD's feast of Booths, which shall continue for seven days. ³⁵On the first day, a declared holy day, you shall do no heavy work. ³⁶For seven days you shall offer an oblation to the LORD, and on the eighth day you will have a declared holy day. You shall offer an oblation to the LORD. It is the festival closing. You shall do no heavy work.

³⁷These, therefore, are the festivals of the LORD which you shall declare holy

---

Most important, the day provides an occasion for necessary atonements that are overlooked by the various sin and purification offerings. There would always be residual sins, both communal and individual, for which the community must render accounts. This day filled the gap. The gravity of this observance comes across in the penalty of being cut off from the community, with God actively removing that person from their midst (23:30). The meaning and message of this day informs our New Testament understanding of Christ's redemptive atonement for the sins of humanity (Heb 8–9).

23:33-44 The feast of Booths

This third fall festival and last of the pilgrimage feasts is sometimes called Tabernacles and lasts for seven days. It celebrates the harvest of grapes and olives, acknowledging the end of the annual agricultural seasons. As a vintage feast it has some parallels with the Greco-Roman feasts of Dionysius/Bacchus. The designation "booths" reflects the shelters built to house the many pilgrims that came to Jerusalem for its observance.

The festiveness of this occasion can hardly be exaggerated. Celebration included candle processions, dancing through the night, and the generous consumption of wine by revelers. Though rooted in celebration of the harvest and an appeal to God for another fruitful season, the festival evolved into a time of anticipating the coming of the Messiah and the independence of Israel (see 2 Macc 1:9-36). This change in focus shows that festivals are very much living traditions, often rooted in one reality and later given other meanings.

days, in order to offer as an oblation to the LORD burnt offerings and grain offerings, sacrifices and libations, as prescribed for each day, ³⁸in addition to the LORD's sabbaths, your donations, your various votive offerings, and the voluntary offerings that you present to the LORD.

³⁹On the fifteenth day, then, of the seventh month, when you have gathered in the produce of the land, you shall celebrate the feast of the LORD for a whole week. The first and the eighth day shall be days of rest. ⁴⁰On the first day you shall gather fruit of majestic trees, branches of palms, and boughs of leafy trees and valley willows. Then for a week

you shall make merry before the LORD, your God. ⁴¹You shall keep this feast of the LORD for one whole week in the year. By perpetual statute throughout your generations in the seventh month of the year, you shall keep it. ⁴²You shall dwell in booths for seven days; every native-born Israelite shall dwell in booths, ⁴³that your descendants may realize that, when I led the Israelites out of the land of Egypt, I made them dwell in booths. I, the LORD, am your God.

⁴⁴Thus did Moses announce to the Israelites the festivals of the LORD.

24 The Sanctuary Light. ¹The LORD said to Moses: ²Order the Israelites

The colorful information in verses 39-43 deserves comment. The Hebrews camped in temporary shelters on their exodus journey to the Promised Land. They were a people "on the move." Now enjoying the abundance of the land, the people reenact that simple living with memory and gratitude. On their minds would be words like those from Psalm 136:10-12: "Who struck down the firstborn of Egypt, / for his mercy endures forever; / And led Israel from their midst, / for his mercy endures forever; / With mighty hand and an outstretched arm, / for his mercy endures forever."

Most people live by a daily calendar, caught up in routines and deadlines, places to go and people to see. Reading about holy days in Leviticus offers hermeneutical insights for the modern reader. First, men and women in ministerial leadership will probably better relate to these observances. Their lives are caught up in church duties and presiding at ceremonies. Second, Leviticus invites the laity to reflect on their personal calendar. Are weekly observances in a faith tradition—sabbath, Sunday, etc.—more than interruptions? Are these days simply obligations to fulfill or are they moments of rest and grace? Third, Old Testament rituals remind us that liturgy means celebration of the gifts of creation. Beneath the many details of observance in ancient Israel lie values that speak to holy worship in any faith tradition.

24:1-4 The sanctuary light

Care of the sanctuary lamp follows nicely from the previous section because olive oil, a gift of the autumn harvest, is involved. The first extraction of

to bring you clear oil of crushed olives for the light, so that you may keep the lamp burning regularly. ³In the tent of meeting, outside the veil that hangs in front of the covenant, Aaron shall set up the lamp to burn before the Lord regularly, from evening till morning, by a perpetual statute throughout your generations. ⁴He shall set up the lamps on the pure gold menorah to burn regularly before the Lord.

The Showbread. ⁵You shall take bran flour and bake it into twelve cakes, using two tenths of an ephah of flour for each cake. ⁶These you shall place in two piles, six in each pile, on the pure gold table before the Lord. ⁷With each pile put some pure frankincense, which shall serve as an oblation to the Lord, a token of the bread offering. ⁸Regularly on each sabbath day the bread shall be set out before the Lord on behalf of the Israelites by an everlasting covenant. ⁹It shall belong to Aaron and his sons, who must eat it in a sacred place, since it is most sacred, his as a perpetual due from the oblations to the Lord.

Punishment of Blasphemy. ¹⁰A man born of an Israelite mother and an Egyptian father went out among the Israelites, and in the camp a fight broke out between the son of the Israelite woman

---

oil was the purest and most valuable. Modern terminology uses "extra virgin" to describe this squeezing. The purest and clearest of oil was typically used for cooking and medicinal purposes. Later presses of oil were for lighting lamps and other secondary functions. The stipulation of clear oil indicates that only the best was fit for the sanctuary, setting the holy place apart from household use of oil for lighting, medicinal needs, and other purposes.

24:5-9 The showbread

Bread offerings to gods are evidenced throughout ancient Near Eastern cultures. However, the showbread or bread of the presence in the Israelite temple was not to feed God but to represent the offering of a staple of life (see Exod 25:23-30). The twelve loaves or cakes represent the twelve tribes in covenant with God. The placement of the bread so near the holy of holies affirms its holiness and being set apart to God. The story in 1 Samuel 21:2-8 where David and his soldiers eat the showbread comes to mind. Such a bold action would be an abomination except for the fact that they were in a state of holiness, having refrained from sexual activity during time of war (cf. Mark 2:23-28).

24:10-23 Punishment of blasphemy, and the *lex talionis*

Blasphemy is essentially cursing God. Although a curse may be a personal act, there is a communal element to such a transgression that calls for a communal response. The power of invoking a divine name and the efficacy of blessings and curses were powerful in the mind of the ancients.

and an Israelite man. [11]The son of the Israelite woman uttered the LORD's name in a curse and blasphemed. So he was brought to Moses—now his mother's name was Shelomith, daughter of Dibri, of the tribe of Dan— [12]and he was kept in custody till a decision from the LORD should settle the case for them. [13]The LORD then said to Moses: [14]Take the blasphemer outside the camp, and when all who heard him have laid their hands on his head, let the whole community stone him. [15]Tell the Israelites: Anyone who blasphemes God shall bear the penalty; [16]whoever utters the name of the LORD in a curse shall be put to death. The whole community shall stone that person; alien and native-born alike must be put to death for uttering the LORD's name in a curse.

[17]Whoever takes the life of any human being shall be put to death; [18]whoever takes the life of an animal shall make restitution of another animal, life for a life. [19]Anyone who inflicts a permanent injury on his or her neighbor shall receive the same in return: [20]fracture for fracture, eye for eye, tooth for tooth. The same injury that one gives another shall be inflicted in return. [21]Whoever takes the life of an animal shall make restitution, but whoever takes a human life shall be put to death. [22]You shall have but one rule, for alien and native-born alike. I, the LORD, am your God.

[23]When Moses told this to the Israelites, they took the blasphemer outside the camp and stoned him; they did just as the LORD commanded Moses.

Hence, to curse another person in God's name bespeaks assuming a prerogative not given to humans. Who can dare to assume for oneself what God can or will do? Who can coerce God to fulfill a curse? To curse God directly is thus a capital offense.

The damning nature of blasphemy relates well to the so-called *lex talionis*: an eye for an eye, a tooth for a tooth. Punishments for violent acts must be proportional to the damage and not in excess. In sum, curses are often emotional and disproportionate, so excess must be avoided in acts of retribution as the *lex talionis* demands (cf. Matt 5:38-42).

The principle of equality also informs our understanding of the *lex talionis*. In an unfair world the wealthy can buy themselves out of a crime, while the poor must serve their time. This law provides no monetary or other material compensation for damages against another person. All must make equal restitution for the same crime. Further, this law demonstrates that violations against the sanctuary do not stand over and above violations of daily life. God's holiness pervades every aspect of life. Violence against one's neighbor is violence against the God in whose nature that person is made. To strike and injure another person for no justifiable reason evokes divine judgment. One must act under the law and not out of unbridled anger or vigilante justice.

25 **The Sabbatical Year.** [1]The LORD said to Moses on Mount Sinai: [2]Speak to the Israelites and tell them: When you enter the land that I am giving you, let the land, too, keep a sabbath for the LORD. [3]For six years you may sow your field, and for six years prune your vineyard, gathering in their produce. [4]But during the seventh year the land shall have a sabbath of complete rest, a sabbath for the LORD, when you may neither sow your field nor prune your vineyard. [5]The aftergrowth of your harvest you shall not reap, nor shall you pick the grapes of your untrimmed vines. It shall be a year of rest for the land. [6]While the land has its sabbath, all its produce will be food to eat for you yourself and for your male and female slave, for your laborer and the tenant who live with you, [7]and likewise for your livestock and for the wild animals on your land.

The Jubilee Year. [8]You shall count seven weeks of years—seven times seven years—such that the seven weeks of years amount to forty-nine years. [9]Then, on the tenth day of the seventh month let the ram's horn resound; on this, the Day of Atonement, the ram's horn blast shall resound throughout your land. [10]You shall treat this fiftieth year as sacred. You shall proclaim liberty in the land for all its inhabitants. It shall be a jubilee for you, when each of you shall return to your own property, each of you to your own family. [11]This fiftieth year is your year of jubilee; you shall not sow, nor shall you reap the aftergrowth or pick the untrimmed vines, [12]since this is the jubilee. It shall be sacred for you. You may only eat what the field yields of itself.

[13]In this year of jubilee, then, each of you shall return to your own property.

25:1-22 The sabbatical and jubilee years

These observances represent a time of rest and release. God's rest after creation and the memory of slavery in Egypt are the theological foundations of sabbath and jubilee (cf. Exod 20:8-11; 31:12-17; Deut 5:12-15). The laws cited here emphasize rest for the land and care of the poor. Such a reprieve may have been more an ideal than a practice, given the delicate balance of feast and famine in ancient Palestine. Most people eked out a daily living and had little time for a day of rest. Crops had to be managed and animals tended to.

Whatever the socio-cultural realities, the value of a time of rest enjoys an enduring theological meaning. This meaning includes the call to be compassionate as God is so. Such virtue includes stewardship of creation and relief for the poor. Further, sabbath and jubilee embody the spirit of *shālôm* (peace). Peace in Israelite thought was more than the absence of war; it bespoke harmony and welfare in every facet of life. Leviticus 25 envisions a world in which labor is embraced as a gift, people can rest as needed, and no family lacks hearth and home.

¹⁴Therefore, when you sell any land to your neighbor or buy any from your neighbor, do not deal unfairly with one another. ¹⁵On the basis of the number of years since the last jubilee you shall purchase the land from your neighbor; and so also, on the basis of the number of years of harvest, that person shall sell it to you. ¹⁶When the years are many, the price shall be so much the more; when the years are few, the price shall be so much the less. For it is really the number of harvests that the person sells you. ¹⁷Do not deal unfairly with one another, then; but stand in fear of your God. I, the LORD, am your God.

¹⁸Observe my statutes and be careful to keep my ordinances, so that you will dwell securely in the land. ¹⁹The land will yield its fruit and you will eat your fill, and live there securely. ²⁰And if you say, "What shall we eat in the seventh year, if we do not sow or reap our crop?" ²¹I will command such a blessing for you in the sixth year that there will be crop enough for three years, ²²and when you sow in the eighth year, you will still be eating from the old crop; even into the ninth year, until the crop comes in, you will still be eating from the old crop.

Redemption of Property. ²³The land shall not be sold irrevocably; for the land is mine, and you are but resident aliens and under my authority. ²⁴Therefore, in every part of the country that you occupy, you must permit the land to be redeemed. ²⁵When one of your kindred is reduced to poverty and has to sell some property, that person's closest relative, who has the duty to redeem it, shall come and redeem what the relative has sold. ²⁶If, however, the person has no relative to redeem it, but later on acquires sufficient means to redeem it, ²⁷the person shall calculate the years since the sale, return the balance to the one to whom it was sold, and thus regain the property. ²⁸But if the person

---

The jubilee year is a grand ideal. At that time land held in debt was returned to its heirs, and those enslaved to pay off debts were freed. The theological meaning of this year is noteworthy. The land ultimately belongs to God, and the people must remember the heritage of having been slaves in Egypt (v. 23).

The modern reader may see the very idea of jubilee as poor fiscal policy, but the spirit of jubilee remains timeless. No one has a right to hold permanently what belongs rightfully to another. No one must lock other persons in a cycle of debt from which they cannot break. Our understanding of jubilee in the Old Testament informs the New Testament parable about writing off debts and showing compassion toward those who owe us (see Matt 18:21-35). Show compassion, and judge not lest you be judged (Jas 2:12-13).

25:23-55 Redemption of property

This section elaborates on specific circumstances that concretize the ideals of sabbath and jubilee. The land belongs to the Lord (v. 23); family

does not acquire sufficient means to buy back the land, what was sold shall remain in the possession of the purchaser until the year of the jubilee, when it must be released and returned to the original owner.

²⁹When someone sells a dwelling in a walled town, it can be redeemed up to a full year after its sale—the redemption period is one year. ³⁰But if such a house in a walled town has not been redeemed at the end of a full year, it shall belong irrevocably to the purchaser throughout the generations; it shall not be released in the jubilee. ³¹However, houses in villages that are not encircled by walls shall be reckoned as part of the surrounding farm land; they may be redeemed, and in the jubilee they must be released.

³²In levitical cities the Levites shall always have the right to redeem the houses in the cities that are in their possession. ³³As for levitical property that goes unredeemed—houses sold in cities of their possession shall be released in the jubilee; for the houses in levitical cities are their possession in the midst of the Israelites. ³⁴Moreover, the pasture land belonging to their cities shall not be sold at all; it must always remain their possession.

³⁵When one of your kindred is reduced to poverty and becomes indebted to you, you shall support that person like a resident alien; let your kindred live with you. ³⁶Do not exact interest in advance or accrued interest, but out of fear of God let your kindred live with you. ³⁷Do not give your money at interest or your food at a profit. ³⁸I, the Lᴏʀᴅ, am your God, who brought you out of the land of Egypt to give you the land of Canaan and to be your God.

³⁹When your kindred with you, having been so reduced to poverty, sell themselves to you, do not make them work as slaves. ⁴⁰Rather, let them be like laborers or like your tenants, working with you until the jubilee year, ⁴¹when, together with any children, they shall be released from your service and return to their family and to their ancestral property. ⁴²Since they are my servants, whom I brought out of the land of Egypt, they

---

land must revert to its intended heirs (v. 28); the Levites traditionally hold a special position among the tribes because no parcel of land in Canaan was given to them (Num 18:21-24; Deut 18:1-4). The Levites supported themselves by ritual services and have a perpetual right to their property (v. 32). Further, Israelite countrymen may be pressed into service but not remain slaves in perpetuity (v. 39-43). Non-Israelite slaves bought from neighboring nations may be held in perpetuity (v. 44-46). Israelite slaves must eventually be redeemed by the next of kin (vv. 46-49).

The reason for these laws stems from the memory of Egypt: ". . . whom I brought out of the land of Egypt, I, the Lᴏʀᴅ, your God" (v. 55). The Lord is the creator and redeemer who led the Israelites out of Egypt and later out of Babylon. No permanent captivity can be found in the divine plan for Israel, and neither must it endure in Israelite society. No land and no

shall not sell themselves as slaves are sold. ⁴³Do not lord it over them harshly, but stand in fear of your God.

⁴⁴The male and female slaves that you possess—these you shall acquire from the nations round about you. ⁴⁵You may also acquire them from among the resident aliens who reside with you, and from their families who are with you, those whom they bore in your land. These you may possess, ⁴⁶and bequeath to your children as their hereditary possession forever. You may treat them as slaves. But none of you shall lord it harshly over any of your fellow Israelites.

⁴⁷When your kindred, having been so reduced to poverty, sell themselves to a resident alien who has become wealthy or to descendants of a resident alien's family, ⁴⁸even after having sold themselves, they still may be redeemed by one of their kindred, ⁴⁹by an uncle or cousin, or by some other relative from their family; or, having acquired the means, they may pay the redemption price themselves. ⁵⁰With the purchaser they shall compute the years from the sale to the jubilee, distributing the sale price over these years as though they had been hired as laborers. ⁵¹The more years there are, the more of the sale price

they shall pay back as the redemption price; ⁵²the fewer years there are before the jubilee year, the more they have as credit; in proportion to the years of service they shall pay the redemption price. ⁵³The tenant alien shall treat those who sold themselves as laborers hired on an annual basis, and the alien shall not lord it over them harshly before your very eyes. ⁵⁴And if they are not redeemed by these means, they shall nevertheless be released, together with any children, in the jubilee year. ⁵⁵For the Israelites belong to me as servants; they are my servants, whom I brought out of the land of Egypt, I, the Lᴏʀᴅ, your God.

26 **The Reward of Obedience.** ¹Do not make idols for yourselves. You shall not erect a carved image or a sacred stone for yourselves, nor shall you set up a carved stone for worship in your land; for I, the Lᴏʀᴅ, am your God. ²Keep my sabbaths, and reverence my sanctuary. I am the Lᴏʀᴅ.

³If you live in accordance with my statutes and are careful to observe my commandments, ⁴I will give you your rains in due season, so that the land will yield its crops, and the trees their fruit; ⁵your threshing will last till vintage time, and your vintage till the time for sowing, and you will eat your fill of food, and live

---

people are perpetually lost. Sabbath and jubilees celebrate this vision of harmony and social justice.

26:1-13 The reward of obedience

Leviticus draws to a close with an exhortation to obedience as the path to blessing. Obedience is intimately related to hearing in Israelite thought. To hear means to follow through, to obey (Deut 6:4). The God who frees the Israelites from oppression demands obedience in turn.

securely in your land. ⁶I will establish peace in the land, and you will lie down to rest with no one to cause you anxiety. I will rid the country of ravenous beasts, and no sword shall sweep across your land. ⁷You will rout your enemies, and they shall fall before your sword. ⁸Five of you will put a hundred of your foes to flight, and a hundred of you will put to flight ten thousand, till your enemies fall before your sword. ⁹I will look with favor upon you, and make you fruitful and numerous, as I carry out my covenant with you. ¹⁰You shall eat the oldest stored harvest, and have to discard it to make room for the new. ¹¹I will set my tabernacle in your midst, and will not loathe you. ¹²Ever present in your midst, I will be your God, and you will be my people; ¹³I, the LORD, am your God, who brought you out of the land of Egypt to be their slaves no more, breaking the bars of your yoke and making you walk erect.

The Punishment of Disobedience. ¹⁴But if you do not heed me and do not keep all these commandments, ¹⁵if you reject my statutes and loathe my decrees, refusing to obey all my commandments and breaking my covenant, ¹⁶then I, in turn, will do this to you: I will bring terror upon you—with consumption and fever to dim the eyes and sap the life. You will sow your seed in vain, for your enemies will consume the crop. ¹⁷I will turn against you, and you will be beaten down before your enemies and your foes will lord it over you. You will flee though no one pursues you.

¹⁸If even after this you do not obey me, I will increase the chastisement for your sins sevenfold, ¹⁹to break your proud strength. I will make the sky above you as hard as iron, and your soil as hard as bronze, ²⁰so that your strength will be spent in vain; your land will bear no crops, and its trees no fruit.

²¹If then you continue hostile, unwilling to obey me, I will multiply my blows sevenfold, as your sins deserve. ²²I will unleash wild beasts against you, to rob

---

The path to blessing through obedience is multifaceted. This section offers a variety of ways in a condensed and unsystematic order. The people should reject idols (v. 1) and keep the sabbath (v. 2) so that rain (v. 4) and peace (v. 6) will abide in the land. Freed from placating idols, the people enjoy the patronage of the one God. Freed from endless toil, the people can embrace the rhythmic time of sabbath. Rain provides gifts of the earth, while peace ensures domestic and social order. Divine presence binds these gifts together: one God and one people (v. 12). The Israelites were freed from slavery in Egypt but are now the Lord's servants. Their vassal state is transferred from Pharaoh to the Lord.

26:14-39 The punishment of disobedience

The curses for disobedience are more specific than the blessings for obedience. Further, the repetition of sevenfold penalties punctuates this section (vv. 18, 21, 24, 28), emphasizing the severity of the curses enjoined.

you of your children and wipe out your livestock, till your population dwindles away and your roads become deserted. ²³If, with all this, you still do not accept my discipline and continue hostile to me, ²⁴I, too, will continue to be hostile to you and I, for my part, will smite you for your sins sevenfold. ²⁵I will bring against you the sword, the avenger of my covenant. Though you then huddle together in your cities, I will send pestilence among you, till you are delivered to the enemy. ²⁶When I break your staff of bread, ten women will need but one oven for baking your bread, and they shall dole it out to you by weight; and though you eat, you shall not be satisfied.

²⁷If, despite all this, you disobey and continue hostile to me, ²⁸I will continue in my hostile rage toward you, and I myself will discipline you for your sins sevenfold, ²⁹till you begin to eat the flesh of your own sons and daughters. ³⁰I will demolish your high places, overthrow your incense stands, and cast your corpses upon the corpses of your idols. In my loathing of you, ³¹I will lay waste your cities and desolate your sanctuaries, refusing your sweet-smelling offerings. ³²So devastated will I leave the land that your enemies who come to live there will stand aghast at the sight of it. ³³And you I will scatter among the nations at the point of my drawn sword, leaving your countryside desolate and your cities deserted. ³⁴Then shall the land, during the time it lies waste, make up its lost sabbaths, while you are in the land of your enemies; then shall the land have rest and make up for its sabbaths ³⁵during all the time that it lies desolate, enjoying the rest that you would not let it have on your sabbaths when you lived there.

³⁶Those of you who survive in the lands of their enemies, I will make so fainthearted that the sound of a driven leaf will pursue them, and they shall run as if from the sword, and fall though no one pursues them; ³⁷stumbling over one another as if to escape a sword,

---

The curses begin with the individual and dovetail to the larger community. That God, in turn, will give the people what they deserve reflects the *lex talionis* (24:20): eye for an eye, tooth for tooth.

The mounting gravity of the curses stems from the persistent defiance among the people (vv. 18, 21, 23, 27). God is forced to escalate the curses to such horrors as cannibalism (v. 29) and the destruction of the holy places (v. 31). But eventually the stiff-necked people will give in, even if they be just a remnant of what was before. The survivors will carry their own guilt and sometimes that of their ancestors (v. 39). The notion of sins of the fathers visited on the sons recurs at several points in the Old Testament (Exod 34:6-7; Num 14:18; Jer 5:7; Lam 5:7). Most famous is the proverb in Jeremiah: "The parents ate unripe grapes, / and the children's teeth are set on edge" (31:29; cf. Ezek 18:2).

while no one is after them—so helpless will you be to take a stand against your foes! ³⁸You shall perish among the nations, swallowed up in your enemies' country. ³⁹Those of you who survive will waste away in the lands of their enemies, for their own and their ancestors' guilt.

⁴⁰They will confess their iniquity and the iniquity of their ancestors in their treachery against me and in their continued hostility toward me, ⁴¹so that I, too, had to be hostile to them and bring them into their enemies' land. Then, when their uncircumcised hearts are humbled and they make amends for their iniquity, ⁴²I will remember my covenant with Jacob, and also my covenant with Isaac; and also my covenant with Abraham I will remember. The land, too, I will remember. ⁴³The land will be forsaken by them, that in its desolation without them, it may make up its sabbaths, and that they, too, may make good the debt of their guilt for having spurned my decrees and loathed my statutes. ⁴⁴Yet even so, even while they are in their enemies' land, I will not reject or loathe them to the point of wiping them out, thus making void my covenant with them; for I, the LORD, am their God. ⁴⁵I will remember for them the covenant I made with their forebears, whom I brought out of the land of Egypt before the eyes of the nations, that I might be their God. I am the LORD.

⁴⁶These are the statutes, decrees and laws which the LORD established between himself and the Israelites through Moses on Mount Sinai.

26:40-46 Repentance and return

Restoration of a right relationship with God depends on human contrition and the Lord's remembering of the covenant with the ancestors. The theme of remembering (Hebrew *zākar*) is reiterated in this section (vv. 42, 45) and has a rich tradition through the Old Testament. Remembering harks back to God's saving Noah and his family at the great flood (Gen 8:1) and preserving his line as a remnant of humanity. God also remembers childless women and hears their prayers (Gen 30:22-24 [Rachel]; 1 Sam 1:9-19 [Hannah]). Covenant requires that the Lord remembers the promises made long ago: "Remember! Do not break your covenant with us" (Jer 14:21). Further, Deuteronomic theology demands that the people remember the wonders God has wrought for them through the generations (Deut 5:15; 7:18; 8:1-5).

The land is also important in repentance and return; it must be purified of human sin (v. 43). The land motif also speaks to a theology of exile. The deportation of the people to Babylon gives the Promised Land time to rest and grow back to its fertile self. A later remnant will repopulate the land and live according to God's laws. Remembrance of the Sinai covenant remains foundational to this event (vv. 45-46).

The nine-branched menorah/candelabra used in Jewish worship

V. Redemption of Offerings

27 **Votive Offerings and Dedica-tions.** [1]The LORD said to Moses: [2]Speak to the Israelites and tell them: When anyone makes a vow to the LORD with respect to the value of a human being, [3]the value for males between the ages of twenty and sixty shall be fifty silver shekels, by the sanctuary shekel; [4]and for a female, the value shall be thirty shekels. [5]For persons between the ages of five and twenty, the value for a male shall be twenty shekels, and for a female, ten shekels. [6]For persons between the ages of one month and five years, the value for a male shall be five silver shekels, and for a female, three shekels. [7]For persons of sixty or more, for a male the value shall be fifteen shekels, and ten shekels for a female. [8]However, if the one who made the vow is too poor to meet the sum, the person must be set before the priest, who shall determine a value; the priest will do this in keeping with the means of the one who made the vow.

[9]If the offering vowed to the LORD is an animal that may be sacrificed, every such animal given to the LORD becomes sacred. [10]The offerer shall not substitute or exchange another for it, either a worse or a better one. If the offerer exchanges one animal in place of another, both the original and its substitute shall become sacred. [11]If any unclean animal which is unfit for sacrifice to the LORD is vowed, it must be set before the priest, [12]who shall determine its value in keeping with its good or bad qualities, and the value set by the priest shall stand. [13]If the offerer wishes to redeem the animal, the person shall pay one fifth more than this valuation.

[14]When someone dedicates a house as sacred to the LORD, the priest shall determine its value in keeping with its

---

REDEMPTION OF OFFERINGS

Leviticus 27

Most commentators consider this chapter an appendix to Leviticus. Numerous vows and related gifts to the Lord are discussed. These gifts can be persons or property and involve a serious commitment that can only be annulled in special cases. Several Old Testament passages warn against making impulsive or frivolous vows: "When you make a vow to the LORD, your God, you shall not delay in fulfilling it; for the LORD, your God, will surely require it of you and you will be held guilty" (Deut 23:22; cf. Eccl 5:3-6; Sir 18:22-23). The payment scale in shekels, estimated by age and gender, is so high that it would deter the average person from making rash and imprudent vows. The amounts cited in each case bespeak that person's ability to redeem a votive offering, i.e., small children and seniors over sixty years old produce less service. It is also noteworthy that the distinctions in payments do not figure in wealth and social status. All persons are suitable gifts to the Lord who sees into the heart and is not swayed by worldly power and status.

good or bad qualities, and the value set by the priest shall stand. [15]A person dedicating a house who then wishes to redeem it shall pay one fifth more than the price thus established, and then it will again belong to that individual.

[16]If someone dedicates to the LORD a portion of hereditary land, its valuation shall be made according to the amount of seed required to sow it, the acreage sown with a homer of barley seed being valued at fifty silver shekels. [17]If the dedication of a field is made at the beginning of a jubilee period, the full valuation shall hold; [18]but if it is some time after this, the priest shall estimate its money value according to the number of years left until the next jubilee year, with a corresponding reduction on the valuation. [19]A person dedicating a field who then wishes to redeem it shall pay one fifth more than the price thus established, and so reclaim it. [20]If, instead of redeeming such a field, one sells it to another, it may

no longer be redeemed; [21]but at the jubilee it shall be released as sacred to the LORD; like a field that is put under the ban, it shall become priestly property.

[22]If someone dedicates to the LORD a field that was purchased and was not part of hereditary property, [23]the priest shall compute its value in proportion to the number of years until the next jubilee, and on the same day the person shall pay the price thus established, a sacred donation to the LORD; [24]at the jubilee the field shall revert to the hereditary owner of this land from whom it had been purchased.

[25]Every valuation shall be made according to the standard of the sanctuary shekel. There are twenty gerahs to the shekel.

Irredeemable Offerings. [26]Note that a firstborn animal, which as such already belongs to the LORD, may not be dedicated. Whether an ox or a sheep, it is the LORD's. [27]But if it is an unclean animal,

---

The dedication of house or land (vv. 14-24) sets that property apart for sacred purposes. The offering need not be permanent. The owner can redeem the property for a certain fee. The most colorful example of this principle occurs in Ruth 4:1-12. Boaz redeems the property of his deceased kinsman, Elimelech, in a protracted episode set at the city gate before assembled elders. Boaz must also take Ruth (daughter-in-law of Elimelech and widow of his son Mahlon) as his wife and so continue that family line. His action shows his love for Ruth and respect for due process.

Mention of the jubilee year shows that inheritances must not be permanently taken from a family, even for cultic purposes. This provision bespeaks the spirit of the prophets who railed against kings and creditors permanently seizing the rightful inheritance of others, especially the poor (e.g., Isa 5:8-10; Mic 2:1-3). Ancient empires were known to seize tracts of land to build temples and related structures. Though sometimes engaging in such practices, Israel is warned not to do so. Such is an egregious injustice.

it may be redeemed by paying one fifth more than its value. If it is not redeemed, it shall be sold at its value.

²⁸Note, also, that any possession which someone puts under the ban for the LORD, whether it is a human being, an animal, or a hereditary field, shall be neither sold nor redeemed; everything that is put under the ban becomes most holy to the LORD. ²⁹All human beings that are put under the ban cannot be redeemed; they must be put to death.

³⁰All tithes of the land, whether in grain from the fields or in fruit from the trees, belong to the LORD; they are sacred to the LORD. ³¹If someone wishes to redeem any of the tithes, the person shall pay one fifth more than their value. ³²The tithes of the herd and the flock, every tenth animal that passes under the herdsman's rod, shall be sacred to the LORD. ³³It shall not matter whether good ones or bad ones are thus chosen, and no exchange may be made. If any exchange is made, both the original animal and its substitute become sacred and cannot be redeemed.

³⁴These are the commandments which the LORD gave Moses on Mount Sinai for the Israelites.

The property of a person given in vow to the Lord cannot be sold or ransomed (vv. 28-29). The Hebrew term used here (*ḥērem*, a ban) has various meanings in the Old Testament, including things banned from use by God or peoples doomed to destruction. For example, Deuteronomy bans or dooms the indigenous peoples of Canaan as the Israelites engage in conquest (20:15-18). Here the ban (things "doomed" to the Lord) must remain in perpetuity for the gift is consecrated and set apart to God.

Tithes (vv. 30-33) in the Old Testament took on various expressions and served a variety of sacred purposes. Some offerings went to support the Jerusalem temple and sanctuaries. The offering of grain, wine, oil, and firstling animals was typical. Those unable to transport their produce or animals could send a monetary equivalent. Levites were supported from this income as well (Deut 14:22-29). Tithing included an element of social justice. The material goods and monies accrued provided care for the widow, orphan, and alien. The prophets warned that such giving must include the proper inner disposition; lip service while oppressing the poor brings divine judgment (Amos 4:1-5).

Verse 34 concludes Leviticus. As noted above, chapter 27 appears to be an appendix added by a later redactor. The intention behind this addition remains unclear, but Leviticus 27 certainly offers a conclusion that softens the curses in chapter 26. The repetition of "Sinai" serves an *inclusio* with 26:46 and binds these chapters together as narrative.

I would invite the reader to read Psalm 119, the longest in the Psalter, in its entirety as a closing prayer to this commentary on Leviticus: "I long for your salvation, LORD; / and your law is my delight" (v. 174).

REVIEW AIDS AND DISCUSSION TOPICS

Introduction *(pages 5–9)*

1. What values in religious education does Leviticus propose to us? What educational values in Leviticus and the rest of the Scriptures do you find timeless and relevant for today?

2. What source/tradition highly influenced Leviticus and what are the characteristics of this tradition?

3. What are some of the types of biblical criticism that help us understand the meaning and message of Leviticus?

4. Why is holiness such an important theme in Leviticus? How does Leviticus understand holiness? How does that understanding compare with your own?

5. What information in the introduction do you find most interesting as you begin to read the commentary?

Leviticus 1–7 Sacrifices and offerings *(pages 11–28)*

1. What types of sacrifices are described in Leviticus 1–7? How are they offered and what are their benefits?

2. Why is Moses the central figure in Leviticus? How does the book characterize Moses as leader of the Israelites?

3. What is the meaning of blood in the Old Testament? What is the role of sacrificial blood in Leviticus?

4. What is the symbolic value of ashes, fire, fat, and other objects in Leviticus? What similar items are essential to the liturgy of your faith tradition and what are their meanings? What are some sacred vessels in your faith tradition and what are their meanings?

Leviticus 8–10 Ceremony of ordination *(pages 28–36)*

1. What sets the priest apart from the people in Leviticus? What qualities describe the holy priest? How does the characterization of priesthood relate to your understanding of vocation to serve the Lord? What are the distinctions between the priesthood and the laity in Leviticus? In your faith tradition?

Leviticus 11–16 Laws regarding legal purity *(pages 36–56)*

1. What aspects of purity in Leviticus seem foreign today? What aspects seem timeless? What are some modern taboos and social fears that bespeak the issues and concerns raised in Leviticus? What factors make people isolate others or banish them from the community?

2. How does concern for the poor and marginalized in Leviticus speak to us today? Who are the outcasts of today in need of our charity and care? Who are the "scapegoats" in modern society?

Leviticus 17–26 Code of legal holiness *(pages 56–93)*

1. What does Leviticus teach us about the sanctity of human sexuality? In your opinion what attitudes regarding sexual conduct in Leviticus remain timeless? Which attitudes seem time conditioned and open to reinterpretation? What sexual matters does Leviticus seem to omit or be unaware of, given that time and place?

2. What are the main holy days cited in Leviticus and what are they about? What aspects of holy days and feasts in your faith tradition relate to theirs?

3. How does the ban against the perpetual sale of land speak to modern policies of eminent domain and other civil laws? How can we inculcate a respect for the tradition of inheritance in the modern world?

4. What laws in Leviticus bespeak a good sense of social justice? What does Leviticus tell us about the intimate connection between justices and peace?

5. Think of the annual festivals and feasts you have in your culture and faith tradition. What are their meanings and what rituals are used to celebrate them?

Leviticus 27 Redemption of offerings *(pages 94–96)*

1. How do you see Leviticus 27 as a fitting conclusion to the book?

2. What ongoing questions and new questions do you recognize as helpful to a discussion of Leviticus?

3. What three teachings in Leviticus stand out most in your mind? What three teachings most speak to your sense of morality and dedication to peace and justice?

INDEX OF CITATIONS FROM THE
CATECHISM OF THE CATHOLIC CHURCH

The arabic number(s) following the citation refer(s) to the paragraph number(s) in the *Catechism of the Catholic Church*. The asterisk following a paragraph number indicates that the citation has been paraphrased.

Leviticus

8	1539*	19:2		2811
8:12	436*	19:13		2434*
16:2	433*	19:15		1807
16:15-16	433,* 613*	19:18		2055*
17:14	2260*	20:26		2813
18:7-20	2388*	26:12		2550

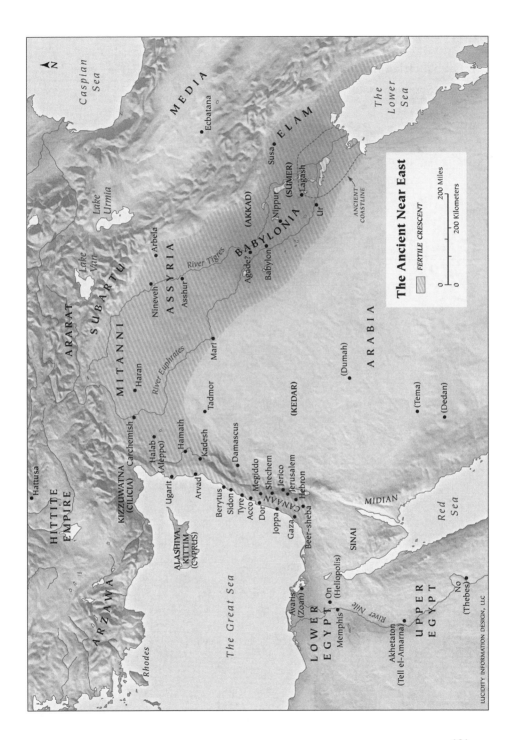

The Ancient Near East

FERTILE CRESCENT

| 0 | 200 Miles |
| 0 | 200 Kilometers |

LUCIDITY INFORMATION DESIGN, LLC

101

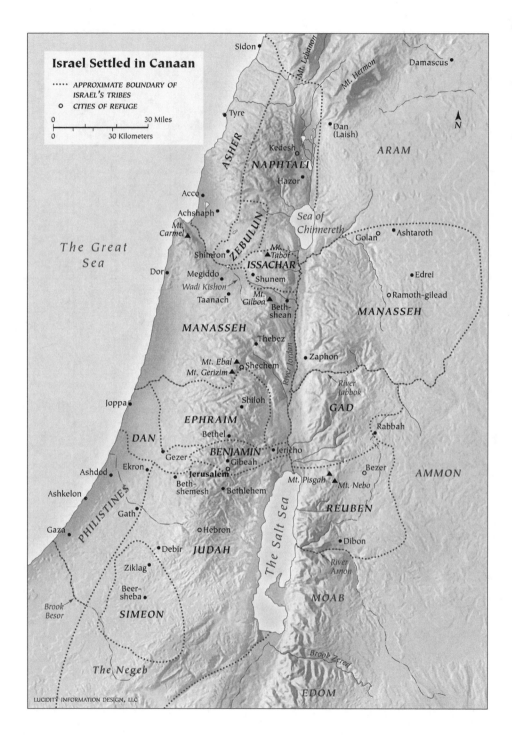

Israel Settled in Canaan

······· APPROXIMATE BOUNDARY OF
            ISRAEL'S TRIBES
    o   CITIES OF REFUGE

0 _____ 30 Miles
0 _____ 30 Kilometers

Sidon

Damascus

Mt. Lebanon

Mt. Hermon

Tyre

Dan
(Laish)

ARAM

Kedesh

NAPHTALI

Hazor

ASHER

Acco

Achshaph

Mt.
Carmel

Sea of
Chinnereth

ZEBULUN

Golan   Ashtaroth

The Great
Sea

Shimron

Mt.
Tabor

ISSACHAR

Edrei

Dor

Megiddo

Shunem

Wadi Kishon

Mt.
Gilboa

Ramoth-gilead

Taanach

Beth-
shean

MANASSEH

MANASSEH

Thebez

Zaphon

River Jordan

Mt. Ebal   Shechem
Mt. Gerizim

River
Jabbok

Joppa

Shiloh

GAD

EPHRAIM

Bethel

Rabbah

DAN

Gezer   BENJAMIN   Jericho
          Gibeah

Ekron   Jerusalem   Bezer

Ashdod   Beth-   AMMON
          shemesh   Bethlehem

Ashkelon   Mt. Pisgah   Mt. Nebo

Gath   REUBEN

Gaza

PHILISTINES   The Salt Sea

Hebron   Dibon

Debir   JUDAH

Ziklag   River
                          Arnon

Beer-
sheba

Brook
Besor   SIMEON   MOAB

The Negeb

EDOM

LUCIDITY INFORMATION DESIGN, LLC

102